New Mexico's Historic Places

New Mexico's

THE GUIDE TO **NATIONAL & STATE REGISTER SITES**

Historic Places

General Editor MARCI L. RISKIN, MAZRIA RISKIN ODEMS, INC.

NEW MEXICO HISTORIC PRESERVATION DIVISION

Foreword ROBERT J. TÓRREZ

OCEAN TREE BOOKS

Adventure Roads Travel

Santa Fe, New Mexico

NEW MEXICO'S HISTORIC PLACES
The Guide to National and State Register Sites

This project was administered by the Historic Preservation Division Office of Cultural Affairs, State of New Mexico, 228 E. Palace Avenue, Santa Fe, New Mexico, 87501.

This publication has been financed in part with federal funds from the National Park Service, U.S. Department of the Interior. However, the contents and opinions do not necessarily reflect the views or policies of the Department of the Interior, nor does the mention of trade names or commercial products constitute endorsement or recommendation by the Department of the Interior.

FOREWORD Robert Tórrez
INTRODUCTION Frances Levine, Ph.D. and Thomas Merlan
HISTORIC PRESERVATION DIVISION DESCRIPTION Lynne Sebastian, Ph.D.
STATE AND NATIONAL REGISTER DESCRIPTIONS Lynne Sebastian, Ph.D.
NATIONAL HISTORIC LANDMARK AND WORLD HERITAGE SITE DESCRIPTIONS Lynne Sebastian, Ph.D.
LABORATORY OF ANTHROPOLOGY DESCRIPTION Jan Biella
HOW TO USE THIS GUIDEBOOK Marci L. Riskin
REGIONAL DESCRIPTIONS Lynne Sebastian, Ph.D.
DESCRIPTIONS OF HIGHLIGHTED PROPERTIES Thomas Merlan and Frances Levine, Ph.D.

GENERAL EDITIOR Marci L. Riskin
BOOK DESIGN Swell Design, Inc.
BOOK PRODUCTION Mazria Riskin Odems, Inc.

Ocean Tree Books
Adventure Roads Travel series
Post Office Box 1295
Santa Fe, New Mexico 87504
(505) 983-1412
www.oceantree.com

ISBN: 0-943734-40-1

Library of Congress CIP data:
New Mexico's historic places: the guide to National and State Register sites / general editor, Marci L. Riskin ; foreword, Robert J. Torrez.
p. cm. – (Adventure roads series)
ISBN 0-943734-40-1
1. Historic sites—New Mexico—Guidebooks. 2. New Mexico—Guidebooks.
3. New Mexico—History, Local. I. Riskin, Marci L.. 1966- II. Series

F797 .N495 2000
917.8904'53—dc21 99-058985

Acknowledgments

The Historic Preservation Division wishes to thank Marci Riskin of Mazria Riskin Odems, Inc., whose energy, enthusiasm and hard work kept this project on track through all its ups and downs; Mary Ann Anders, Ph.D., now retired from the Division and New Mexico's own "keeper" of the National and State Registers, whose dedication and professionalism ensured that many of these properties would be listed; the many dedicated and skilled professionals who have served on the Cultural Properties Review Committee through the years; Frances Levine, Ph.D., and former State Historic Preservation Officer Thomas Merlan, who brought many years of knowledge and a surpassing love for New Mexico's history to this project; and especially the hundreds of public and private owners of the properties described in this book. It is their painstaking, loving care for these places that has preserved them through the years and made them available to us and to future generations of New Mexicans.

We also wish to acknowledge the National Park Service, Department of the Interior, which supports the work of the Division through Historic Preservation Fund grants and which provided the funding used to develop this book.

Finally, I personally would like to thank the staff of the Division who gathered data, answered questions, wrote, rewrote, edited, organized, found photos, and generally provided yeoman service in the preparation of this book. Their talent, dedication, and cheerfulness in the face of adversity was, as always, a source of inspiration to me.

LYNNE SEBASTIAN, PH.D.
State Historic Preservation Officer

Contents

Opposite: Chaves County Courthouse, Roswell

Big Bead Mesa, Sandoval County

Foreword

In 1998, New Mexico observed the 400th anniversary, or *Cuarto Centenario,* of its settlement by colonists led by Don Juan de Oñate in 1598. The year was observed by a great number of activities in many communities throughout the state. But the occasion was not without controversy. A number of New Mexico's Native American tribes were quick to point out that they had lived in this region many centuries before the Spanish arrived and argued that European settlement had negatively impacted these aboriginal peoples in many ways.

The heated dialogue that characterized some Cuarto Centenario activities reminded many of us that humans have found New Mexico an attractive place to live for many centuries. Each of the successive peoples who made their homes along our river valleys and mountains has contributed to our long, varied, and unique cultural heritage. For more than thirty years the State Register of Cultural Properties has been an integral part of identifying, documenting and protecting that cultural heritage. The more than 1700 sites that have been entered on the register to date constitute one of the most comprehensive listings of what it is that makes New Mexico special. It includes such seemingly disparate entries such as Bob Olinger's mundane wallet and the truly spectacular ruins of Chaco Canyon. It allows us to contrast the relatively new technology of Albuquerque's 1950s Solar Building with very old technologies in evidence at Blackwater Draw, where we find the Clovis points used for hunting by some of the earliest New Mexicans. It allows us to trace such divergent roads as the ancient trails leading to the Zuni Salt Lake, the nineteenth century Butterfield Overland Mail Route, and Route 66 over which we got our "kicks."

This publication will make this diverse listing of New Mexico's cultural resources available to the general public for the first time. Not that the listing has ever been a big secret. The register and its supporting documentation is public record and available to anyone who wants to see it. But you had to go to the offices of the New Mexico Historic Preservation Division in Santa Fe to do so. Now each of us can easily see what is listed in each town and county. In doing so, I hope we might become more aware of New Mexico's marvelous cultural treasures as well as remember that there is still a vast amount of work to be done to ensure their survival and enjoyment by future generations.

ROBERT J. TÓRREZ
State Historian
Chairman, Cultural Properties Review Committee

Introduction

New Mexico's Historic Places is a guide to the properties in New Mexico that are listed on the National Register of Historic Places and the State Register of Cultural Properties. It is designed for both visitors to the state and for those fortunate enough to live here, surrounded by the natural beauty and fascinating history of the Land of Enchantment. People have lived in New Mexico for more than 12,000 years, and during that time they have left behind traces of their lives that are preserved today and recognized through listing in the State and National Registers. This guide was prepared under the direction of the State Historic Preservation Division to make information about our history and our historic places more readily available to those interested in the past.

This introduction includes brief summaries of the archaeology and history of New Mexico and information about the Historic Preservation Division and the State and National Registers. The main body of the book is organized by region and includes a complete list of registered properties in that region along with more detailed discussions of selected important properties. A key to using the regional listings is provided at the end of this introduction.

An Overview of New Mexico Archaeology

The earliest people in New Mexico were the hunting groups or bands that archaeologists call the Paleoindians. The first people immigrated into the Southwest about twelve thousand years ago, at the end of the last Ice Age. Paleoindian peoples hunted big game such as camel, bison and mammoth around springs and lake margins in the cool, wet glacial landscape. We know them mainly from the finely worked stone tools and weapons they left behind. The Clovis complex of stone tools and weapons represents the earliest known inhabitants of North America. The Clovis complex was followed by the Folsom complex. The change from Clovis to Folsom, marked by differences in the game hunted and the tools used, may mean that tool and weapon forms changed as the Ice Age mammals died out some 7,000 to 8,000 years ago. Gradually, the climate became warmer and drier, and the technology was modified to adapt to changes in the environment and food sources.

The Paleoindian period was followed by the period and way of life called the Archaic — a culture of mobile, family-centered bands living on a variety of plants and small game. This hunting and gathering way of life was a very successful and stable one that persisted for thousands of years — from about 5500 B.C. to about A.D. 200. In late Archaic times, domestic plants including corn, beans and squash, and later cotton, were brought to New Mexico from farther south in Mexico. Many of the earliest agricultural sites in the Southwest, including Bat Cave and Tularosa Cave, are found in the Mogollon Highlands of southwestern New Mexico. Some of the earliest evidence of the Archaic way of life has been found in these caves. The dry, cool climate of caves has allowed foods, baskets, matting, and intricate textiles of the Archaic peoples to be preserved.

The appearance of villages in the Southwest about A.D. 200 marked a change to a more sedentary way of life. Between about A.D. 200 and 900, villages were established across much of the Greater Southwest. Villagers cultivated corn, beans and squash as well as cotton in some areas, although hunting and gathering of native plants continued to be important long after agriculture was widely adopted in the Southwest. Baskets were made for carrying and storing items, but the use of pottery vessels for cooking and storage became widespread by A.D. 500. The first substantial houses also appeared at this time, first semisubterranean pithouses and later blocks of surface rooms.

The village dwellers of the Southwest have been divided by archaeologists into three major cultural traditions on the basis of similarities and differences in architecture, village plans and distinctive design elements found on pottery. One of these major traditions—the Hohokam people—lived in the sonoran desert of southern Arizona, but the other two—the Anasazi of the Four Corners and northern Rio Grande and the Mogollon of southwestern and south central New Mexico—were very important in the prehistory of New Mexico and were the ancestors of the modern Pueblo people.

Beginning about 900 and continuing until the mid 1100s, both the Anasazi and the Mogollon people in New Mexico built large, elaborate villages—the Chaco towns of the Anasazi and the Mimbres pueblos of the Mogollon. The Mimbres people practiced gravity-fed irrigation and produced an impressive pottery tradition, including both intricate geometric patterns and figurative representations of their way of life. In Chaco Canyon there were no permanent streams to permit irrigation, but the people developed elaborate systems for channeling and capturing runoff from the cliffs and arroyos along the canyon. The Chacoan people developed a hierarchical regional system of towns and smaller villages and an elaborate ceremonial and trade network.

During the 1200s most of the large settlements in the Southwest were at higher elevations—for example, the cliff dwellings and pueblos of Mesa Verde National Park and Bandelier National Monument—or along permanent rivers. Beginning around 1300, there was a major reorganization of the ancestral Pueblo settlements in the Southwest, perhaps owing to a series of droughts that made farming impossible in some areas. People moved into places, such as the Rio Grande Valley, the Chama River and Salinas Basin, that had never before had such large populations. Warfare and political and social realignments may also have contributed to the changes in where people lived. Very large communities were built in the late thirteenth and early fourteenth centuries, such as the registered sites at Frijoles Canyon in Bandelier National Monument; at Puye, an ancestral site of the Santa Clara Pueblo; and at Pecos Pueblo on the eastern frontier of the ancestral Pueblo world. By the 1500s, however, there was another regional shift in settlements. Many people dispersed into smaller settlements including some of the present-day pueblos, as the Spanish called these villages.

Some time around 1400, a new group, the Athabaskan speakers, migrated into the Southwest. Linguistic evidence indicateds that these people originated in far northern homelands in Canada. The Athabaskans became the Navajo and the diverse groups that are known as the Apaches. The Navajo have become the largest American Indian nation, occupying an extensive reservation in the Four Corners. Ancestral Navajo sites listed on the National Register record the many ways in which Navajo people adopted cultural practices of the surrounding Pueblo and European cultures. Apache people now live in thriving reservation communities in Dulce, New Mexico, home of the Jicarilla Apache people, and in southeastern New Mexico around Sierra Blanca, the sacred homeland of the Mescalero Apaches.

A Brief Summary of New Mexico History

In 1539 Europeans came into New Mexico for the first time when a Spanish expedition reached Hawikuh, a Zuni town. A larger expedition returned in 1540 under the command of Francisco Vasquez de Coronado and explored widely, recording observations about the people and lands in parts of New Mexico, Arizona and Kansas. Disappointed by his failure to find gold and silver, Coronado returned south to New Spain, as Mexico was then called. More than two generations passed before the Spanish once again began their explorations of the Far North.

Juan de Oñate, appointed by the king of Spain to be the first governor of New Mexico, established the first Spanish colony in 1598 at the confluence of the Rio Chama and the Rio Grande. There at the Tewa pueblo of San Gabriel de Yungue-Ouinge, Oñate's colonists and a Pueblo labor force built a church and convento and dug an *acequia,* or ditch, for irrigating wheat, fruit trees and other crops that were new to the North. The acequias and some of the crops introduced by the colonists are still essential to New Mexico's agricultural economy today. Over the next eighty-two years, the Spanish expanded their area of settlement. They founded a permanent capital at Santa Fe in 1610 and built a government headquarters, the building we now call the Palace of the Governors. Missions were built in the Pueblo communities, and Pueblo people constructed great churches, such as San Estéban Rey at Acoma and Nuestra Señora de los Angeles at Pecos, for the Franciscan fathers whose purpose was to instruct the Indian people in the Catholic faith.

In 1680 the Pueblo people rose in revolt and drove out the Spanish. The settlers formed a community in exile near present-day Juarez, Mexico

Abo Mission Ruin, Torrance County

and El Paso, Texas. A new governor, Diego de Vargas, fought two difficult campaigns of reconquest—in 1693 and again, after a second revolt, in 1696. New Mexico was resettled as a colony and later became a military department of New Spain, with a governor appointed by the Spanish crown. Hispanic and Pueblo people gradually formed a multicultural, agricultural society in New Mexico. Other Indian people such as the Navajo adopted herding and farming, although they also raided both the pueblos and Hispanic communities. A new group of Plains hunters, the Comanches, came into northeastern New Mexico early in the eighteenth century. Apache, Ute and Comanche groups alternately raided or traded with the Hispanic communities from the eighteenth until the mid-nineteenth century. Despite prevailing poverty, profound isolation from the rest of the world, and frequent raids by Plains groups, the expanding Hispanic society established communities incorporating new towns such as Fernández de Taos and Las Trampas. The eighteenth century saw the growth of Spanish settlements, many of them on lands granted to communities by the Spanish crown, along most of the major drainages of the state.

Some Pueblo and Navajo people took refuge from Hispanic domination and from raids by other Indian groups in canyon fastnesses like Big Bead Mesa. The number of Pueblo people dwindled, owing to diseases, attacks by nomadic Indians, and absorption into the Hispanic population. The Pueblos became a minority about 1780. Nevertheless, the remaining Pueblo villagers supported agricultural enterprises that supplied Hispanic communities as well as themselves. Pueblo communities held an important place in the regional economy throughout the eighteenth century. Slave trade, in which Hispanics captured or bought Navajo, Apache and Plains people (mostly women and children) for use as servants and herders, was another aspect of the eighteenth century economy of New Mexico. Known as *genízaros,* these captives became a distinct subgroup of the colonial population. *Genízaros* settled the more exposed frontier communities like Abiquiu in the north and Belen in the south.

In 1821 Mexico won independence from Spain, and New Mexico became a department of the new nation. The government expanded the area of settlement further through new land grants. New Mexico's deep isolation began to diminish. New Mexicans sold sheep and traded wool, hides, blankets and other goods in California, central Mexico, and the United States. Copper mining began at Santa Rita in southwestern New Mexico about 1800, and gold discoveries in the Ortiz Mountains south of Santa Fe in 1828 and in 1839 led to the establishment of significant mining fields.

Anglo-American traders, trappers and merchants who came down the Santa Fe Trail from Missouri to New Mexico formed a new class of entrepreneurs and landowners. The Mexican government made some land grants to Anglo-Americans, in hopes of promoting development while creating a barrier to U.S. expansion. Some communities, for example La Junta, were founded as a result, but the ambitious nation to the east could not be stopped. The United States invaded New Mexico in 1846, and New Mexico became a U.S. territory in 1850. The Anglo-Americans built forts like Stanton and Union to combat the nomadic Indians, and bought beef from Texas cattle ranchers who began to drive herds to the forts in the 1860s.

The Santa Fe Trail was abandoned when the railroad reached New Mexico in 1879. The railroad brought new settlers, new building materials, new technology such as the windmills that made it possible to farm or ranch in many upland areas, and a growing cash economy. Anglos mined gold and silver in the 1860s, and with the arrival of the railroad and the end of the Indian threat, mining of precious metals and coal became important elements of the territorial and regional economy. The Indian wars finally ended in the 1870s and 1880s, and railroad towns like New Las Vegas, Clayton and Roswell sprang up. New Mexico finally achieved statehood in 1912.

The turn of the century brought many changes to the regional economy. From about 1880 to about 1940, New Mexico became famous for its dry and healthful climate, and thousands of "healthseekers" came from all over the country to spas like Ojo Caliente and Montezuma. The earliest automobile roads in New Mexico appeared in the 1900s, but use of cars and trucks was not widespread until the 1930s, after which there was reduced dependence on the railroads. Because Pueblo and Hispanic people had lost much of the land base required for traditional agricultural and pastoral economies, they gradually came to rely more and more on tourism and wage work, including the revival of traditional arts. Anglo-American artists began settling in New Mexico in the 1890s. They represented a new element of the economy while drawing inspiration from the ancient land and its traditional people. Despite growing change, New Mexico remained multicultural, agricultural and traditional. Hispanic people did not become a minority until the 1940s. In the Depression, many New Mexicans worked for New Deal programs including the Civilian Conservation Corps and the Works Progress Administration, building major public projects, many of which are listed on the National and State Registers. The federal and military presence in our vast and sparsely populated state blossomed with the choice of remote mountains and deserts as the sites of the Manhattan Project at Los Alamos and the test range at White Sands.

On July 16, 1945, the world's first atom bomb was detonated at Trinity Site in the Tularosa Basin, where the Paleoindians had hunted camels and mammoths ten thousand years before. New Mexico, the home of the first Americans, saw the beginning of the atomic age.

The New Mexico Historic Preservation Division

The rich and varied history described above has left behind a great wealth of historic buildings and neighborhoods and objects as well as thousands of archaeological sites. Modern development, neglect, vandalism and natural forces all combine to threaten this historic heritage; it is the mission of the Historic Preservation Division of the state Office of Cultural Affairs to assist the people of New Mexico in preserving at least some portion of our historic and prehistoric sites.

The Division, under the leadership of the State Historic Preservation Officer, provides technical assistance to state and federal agencies, local governments, and private owners to assist them in rehabilitating, stabilizing, and preserving historic properties and protecting archaeological sites. Through tax credits and loans, the Division provides incentives for restoration and reuse of historic places. By carrying out its duties under state and federal preservation laws, the Division attempts to minimize unnecessary damage to and loss of historic properties and prehistoric sites. And through grants and public outreach programs, the Division encourages grass roots support for the preservation of our shared heritage.

One of the most important programs of the Historic Preservation Division is the registration of historic places on the State Register of Cultural Properties and the National Register of Historic Places. The Division prepares nominations to the registers and assists owners of properties in preparing nominations; serves as staff to the state's Cultural Properties Review Committee, which makes decisions about which sites to register; and maintains the records of registered and potentially registerable sites and makes them available to researchers and the public.

The State and National Registers

The State Register of Cultural Properties and the National Register of Historic Places are, in effect, honor rolls — lists of places that have been found to be significant to our history and worthy of preservation. The

National Register, which is maintained by the National Park Service, includes not just the grand and nationally significant historic places, but more modest historic properties of state or even local significance as well. The State Register, which is maintained by the state's Historic Preservation Division, recognizes a broad range of historic buildings, neighborhoods, and villages as significant in New Mexico's history as well as archaeological sites, battlefields, engineering features, routes and trails, and even a few objects and collections of objects.

Properties are placed on the State and National Registers through a nomination process that involves documenting the history, condition, and significance of the place. The nominations are reviewed by the Cultural Properties Review Committee — a governor-appointed board of professional architects, archaeologists, and historians — which places properties on the State Register and recommends them to the National Register. The final decision for national registration is made by the Keeper of the National Register in Washington D.C. Generally, properties must be at least 50 years old and meet a series of criteria about their association with our history in order to be eligible for inclusion on these registers.

There is a persistent mythology about what it means for a place to be listed on the State or National Register. One myth is that places listed on the register are guaranteed permanent preservation. Another is that private property owners' rights are abridged by registration; for example, some owners are concerned that the government will tell them what color they can paint their homes. In fact, registration provides for at least some level of protection from government authorized or funded actions, but does not constrain the private owner in any way, unless some form of locally passed land-use ordinance is tied to register status. One of the most important benefits of registration, beyond the recognition of significance that a National or State Register plaque brings, is that registered properties may be eligible for federal and state rehabilitation tax credits and other preservation incentives.

This book contains a list of all the places in New Mexico that are listed on the State and National Registers. In addition, it includes more detailed information about all of the National Historic Landmarks and a selection of other important properties. New Mexico readers may find that their favorite historic places were not selected for these narratives; they may be included in future editions.

National Historic Landmarks ▲ and World Heritage Sites ◎

In addition to being listed on the State or National Registers, very important historic places can be designated National Historic Landmarks (NHLs) or World Heritage Sites. The National Historic Landmarks program of the National Park Service was created in 1935 as a way of recognizing exceptionally significant historic places in the United States. The program was never intended to be systematic or representative of the whole range of historic places, and the 40 NHLs in New Mexico (all of which are described in this guide) form a rather eclectic group. Although superceded in large part by the National Register of Historic Places, the NHL program is still working to identify and designate exceptional places as NHLs.

Under the provisions of the World Heritage Convention, an international agreement concluded in 1972, the signatory nations identify, recognize and protect cultural and natural properties that are of "outstanding universal value to mankind." Proposals are evaluated by a committee of member nations. Each nation is responsible for protecting and interpreting its own properties, but pledges to work with the other member nations to assist threatened sites. The international effort to rescue the monuments of Abu Simbel in Egypt from the rising waters of the Aswan High Dam is an example of such international preservation efforts.

Currently only three places in New Mexico — Carlsbad Caverns National Park, Chaco Culture National Historic Park, and the Pueblo of Taos — have been recognized as World Heritage Sites.

Laboratory of Anthropology

The Laboratory of Anthropology, located in Santa Fe, opened in 1931 with funds provided by John D. Rockefeller, Jr. to promote research, publication, public education and the welfare of the native populations in the Southwest. Its first Curator of Archaeology was H.P. Mera who brought with him records and pottery collected over several years from over 400 archaeological ruins in New Mexico. Mera had the vision to make these materials available to researchers and interested amateurs, and the Laboratory became a clearinghouse and repository for ongoing research and surveys throughout New Mexico. As Mera's collections were analyzed and catalogued, the location of each archaeological ruin was plotted on a map and given a distinct "LA" or Laboratory of Anthropology number. Most other states use the Smithsonian numbering system, but in New Mexico, in keeping with Mera's tradition, each archaeological site recorded, over 120,000 to date, is assigned an LA number. Pindi Pueblo near Santa Fe is LA 1, and the Trinity Site National Historic Landmark, Ground Zero, is LA 100,000.

How to Use This Guidebook

New Mexico's Historic Places: The Guide to National and State Register Sites is designed as a walking and driving guide to New Mexico's cultural heritage, to enhance the experience of the state for residents or those who are traveling through the area. The guidebook includes a complete list of both National Register and State Register properties through 1997.

Most of the properties on the State and National Registers are owned by private entities and are located on private property. Some, particularly archaeological sites, are quite fragile. Although addresses and location information are given in many cases, please respect the rights of property owners and the sensitivity of the properties. Visit only historic districts and sites that are open to the public.

The guide is arranged by region (Northwest, North-Central, Northeast, Central, Southwest and Southeast) and, within these regions, alphabetically by city or town. The regional list is followed by a list of Roads, Trails and Routes on the State Register.

ABBREVIATIONS

Ave.	Avenue
Blvd.	Boulevard
Cir.	Circle
CR	County Road
Dr.	Drive
E	East
ENMU	Eastern New Mexico University
FR	Forest Road
LA	Laboratory of Anthropology
Ln.	Lane
N	North
NE	Northeast
NM	New Mexico Highway
NMHU	New Mexico Highlands University
NMIMT	New Mexico Institute of Mining and Technology
NMSD	New Mexico School for the Deaf
NMSU	New Mexico State University
NMSVH	New Mexico School for the Visually Handicapped
NNMCC	Northern New Mexico CommunityCollege
NR	National Register
NW	Northwest
Pl.	Place
Rd.	Road
S	South
SE	Southeast
SR	State Register
St.	Street
SW	Southwest
US	United States Highway
UNM	University of New Mexico
W	West
WNMU	Western New Mexico University

SYMBOLS

- National Historic Landmark
- World Heritage Site
- Multiple Property Listing

Step 1 Locate the region that is of interest. There are six regions. The map at the beginning of each region show the State Register (SR) numbers of properties which are highlighted within the text.

Step 2 Locate the town or city that is of interest. These are arranged alphabetically within each region. All towns and cities used in addresses can be found in the *Official Highway Map of New Mexico: America's Land of Enchantment,* issued by the New Mexico State Highway and Transportation Department and the New Mexico Department of Tourism. The listings within each town or city are either in that specific town or city or in its vicinity.

Step 3 Each property listing follows a similar format. The first line of the listing contains the name of the property and, in parentheses, other names by which the property is known. If no name is listed, the property is known only by its address. Archaeological properties are also known by their LA (Laboratory of Anthropology) numbers.

Step 4 Determine whether a property is a National Historic Landmark ▲ or World Heritage Site ◉. The symbols are included on the first line of the listing.

Step 5 Find the specific location of the property. Some properties are specifically located with a street name and number. Others have a general location. This is not an indication of whether a property is open to the public or not. Use your best judgment when determining whether or not it is appropriate to visit a property and respect the rights of individual property owners.

Step 6 Find the State Register Number and the year the property was listed on the State Register. This is on the last line of a listing. If a State Register (SR) number appears without an associated year, the property has a State Register number, but is not yet on the State Register.

Step 7 Find the National Register Number and the year the property was listed on the National Register. This is on the last line of a listing following the State Register number. If no National Register (NR) number appears, the property is not on the National Register.

Step 8 Determine if the property is within a historic or archaeological district. The name of the district will follow the SR and NR numbers. All districts are listed on the State or National Register and can be found using the same procedure for locating individual properties.

Step 9 Determine if the property is part of a Multiple Property Listing. These listings are general categories encompassing several properties that are listed on the register separately. Properties which are part of a Multiple Property Listing will display the ☒ symbol followed by the Multiple Property Listing's State Register number. Find the complete list of Multiple Property Listings in the back of the guidebook. Match the number after the ☒ symbol to this numerical list.

Northwest

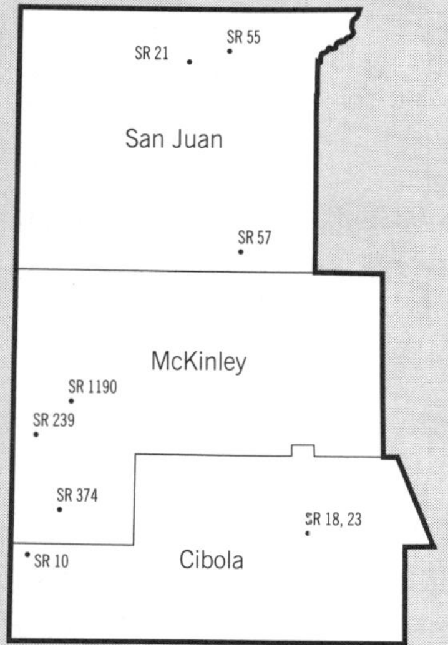

The Northwestern region of New Mexico comprises the piñon and juniper covered mesas of the Colorado Plateau, the San Juan River and its tributaries, the sage plains of the San Juan Basin, the red rock canyons of the Red Mesa Valley, and the high country of the Chuska and Zuni Mountains and Mount Taylor. The region is indelibly associated with Native American cultures, both ancient and modern. It contains the heartland of the prehistoric people known as the Chaco Anasazi, the Dinetah or traditional homeland of the Navajo, a large part of the modern Navajo Nation, and the ancient and modern homes of the pueblos of Acoma, Laguna and Zuni. Not surprisingly, the State and National Register listings in the northwest region are dominated by prehistoric and historic Native American sites, but ranching, farming, oil and gas exploration and development, and the tourist industry associated with the railroads and with Route 66 are represented on the registers as well.

Acoma *(Cibola County)*

Acoma Pueblo

SR #18 (1968), NR #66000500 (1966)

With a date of origin as early as about A.D. 1200 and in-migrations to the area during the drought of 1276-1299, Acoma Pueblo may be the oldest continuously occupied community in the United States. Acoma ancestors comprise at least four different groups: one goes back to early prehistoric times, two are believed to have migrated from the Cebollita region and another is from the Mesa Verde area. The pueblo is on a mesa about 220 feet high (not 357 feet as often stated) and about 70 acres in area. It is composed of three parallel east-west roomblocks, each about 220 yards long and 25 to 30 feet wide. An early Spanish observer noted that the roomblocks rose three or four stories, with small selenite windows and no exterior doors. Access to the rooms was by ladders and rooftop hatches. In 1599 Spanish colonizer Juan de Oñate ordered an attack on the pueblo in retaliation for the death of his nephew in a skirmish there; 800 Acomas were killed and a number taken as slaves. Much of the pueblo was destroyed in the battle; it was rebuilt in adobe in the 17th century. During this period the mission and ancillary structures of San Estéban Rey were built. Until about 1939 when a road was completed, there was no access

to the mesa top, except by footpaths and ladders. Most of the upper stories of the buildings have now been removed, and modern windows and doors have been added. Although the pueblo has been more ceremonial center than actual residence in the 20th century, some families alternate in residence on the mesa by official requirement or on a voluntary basis. Acoma is a principal source of Pueblo building traditions that underlie the Pueblo Revival style. Guided tours begin at the visitor center below the mesa.

San Estevan de Acoma Mission Church (San Estevan del Rey Mission Church)

SR #23 (1968), NR #70000417 (1970)

Acoma Pueblo's mission church of San Estéban Rey and its adjacent convento were built during the years 1629-1641 under the supervision of Fray Juan Ramírez, the first resident Franciscan missionary, who was assigned to Acoma around 1629 to convert the Indians of Acoma to Christianity. The church is about 145 by 45 feet in exterior dimension. Its walls are thirty feet high (and may originally have been higher) and are approximately 6 feet thick. Flanking towers with open belfries add another 25 feet to the height of the facade. The nave is a single space, without transepts or clerestory. Pine *vigas,* beams that support the roof, are 50 feet long and hewn 14 inches square. These beams were cut in the San Mateo Mountains and hand-carried to the mesa top up footpaths and ladders. The *convento,* contiguous to the church's north wall, is a square of rooms and cloister around an interior patio-garden. The *camposanto* in front of the church was created by building retaining masonry walls, including the 45-foot high east wall, and filling them with dirt brought up from below the mesa in baskets. In the mid 1920s, the traditional dirt roof of the church was replaced with concrete, and the facade and north and south towers were repaired using plans and materials provided by the Committee for the Preservation and Restoration of the New Mexico Mission Churches and Acoma labor. The Historic Preservation Division made a series of grants in the 1970s for repairs to the retaining wall of the *camposanto,* the church itself and the adjacent *convento.*

Aztec *(San Juan County)*

H.D. Abrams House

403 North Church Street

SR #876 (1982), NR #85000322 (1985), ⊠ 1716

American Hotel
300 South Main Street
SR #878 (1982), NR #85000323 (1985), ⊠ 1716

Austin/McDonald House
501 Rio Grande
SR #1102 (1984), NR #85000324 (1985), ⊠ 1716

Aztec Main Street Historic District
West side of Main Street between Chuska and Chaco
SR #879 (1982), NR #85000321 (1985), ⊠ 1716

Aztec Motor Company Building
301 South Main Street
SR #1101 (1984), NR #85000325 (1985), ⊠ 1716

Aztec Presbyterian Church
215 North Church Street
SR #716 (1979), CHURCH AVENUE/LOVERS LANE HISTORIC DISTRICT, ⊠ 1716

Aztec Ruins Administration Building/Museum
Aztec Ruins National Monument
SR #1713, NR #96001041 (1996)

Aztec Ruins National Monument
SR #55 (1969), NR #66000484 (1966)

The Aztec Ruins National Monument is located on a gravel terrace above the Animas River, about sixty-five miles north of Chaco Canyon. The site was well-known by the local population and was severely looted various times by pothunters before it was first excavated by archaeologist Earl H. Morris. Morris both lived and worked on site; the visitor center/museum incorporates the Pueblo Revival style building Morris designed for use as a home and office. Aztec is an E-shaped Chacoan great house, with 350-400 rooms and more than two dozen kivas, built between A.D. 1111 and A.D. 1115. The original inhabitants left the Chacoan great house at Aztec around 1175 or 1200, but around 1225, people of the Mesa Verde tradition reoccupied the pueblo, and built another pueblo known as East Ruin. The Aztec Ruins site includes the stabilized West Ruin, which offers an interpretation of Anasazi life and ceremony, the partly excavated East Ruin, the unexcavated Earl Morris Ruin, the excavated Hubbard tri-wall site, and at least six other unexcavated sites or ruins within the Monument's 27 acres.

D. C. Ball House
300 San Juan
SR #1097 (1984), NR #85000326 (1985), ⊠ 1716

Fred Bunker House
115 N. Mesa Verde
SR #875 (1982), CHURCH AVENUE/LOVERS LANE HISTORIC DISTRICT, ⊠ 1716

Maurice Case House
103 N. Mesa Verde
SR #877, CHURCH AVENUE/LOVERS LANE HISTORIC DISTRICT, ⊠ 1716

Church Avenue/Lovers Lane Historic District
Bounded by Rio Grande, Zia, Park and NM 550
SR #1095 (1984), NR 85000329 (1985), ☒ 1716

Daws/Keys House
421 N. Church
SR #1104 (1984), NR #85000330 (1985), ☒ 1716

Denver and Rio Grande Western Railway Depot
314 Rio Grande
SR #1099 (1984), NR #85000331 (1985), ☒ 1716

Engleman/Thomas Building
200 S. Main
SR #1107 (1984), NR #85000332 (1985), ☒ 1716

Lower Animas Ditch
From Church Ave. to Lovers Ln.
SR #1100 (1984), NR #87001116 (1987), ☒ 1716

McCoy/Maddox House
Corner of Maddox and Aztec Blvd.
SR #1096 (1984), NR #85000334 (1985), ☒ 1716

Harvey McCoy House
725 Pioneer
SR #1098 (1984), NR #85000333 (1985), ☒ 1716

James McGee House
501 Sabena St.
SR #1105 (1984), NR #85000335 (1985), ☒ 1716

202 Park Avenue
SR #1106 (1984), NR #85000328 (1985), ☒ 1716

500 White Avenue
SR #1103 (1984), NR #85000327 (1985), ☒ 1716

Blanco *(San Juan County)*
SEE ALSO NORTH-CENTRAL REGION

Christmas Tree Ruin (LA 11097)
SR #361 (1975), NR #86003646 (1987), ☒ 1718

Cottonwood Divide Site (LA 55829)
SR #1356 (1986), NR #86003644 (1987), ☒ 1718

Hadlock's Crow Canyon No. 1 (LA 55830)
SR #1357 (1986), NR #86003642 (1987), CROW CANYON ARCHAEOLOGICAL DISTRICT, ☒ 1718

Halfway House Archaeological Site (LA 15191)
SR #686 (1978), NR #80002565 (1980), ☒ 657

Pierre's Archaeological District (LA 35423, LA 16508)
SR #690 (1978), ☒ 657

Prieta Mesa Site (LA 11251)
SR #1347 (1986), NR #86003647 (1987), ☒ 1718

Simon Canyon (LA 5047)
SR #370 (1975), NR #86003645 (1987), ☒ 1718

Star Rock Refuge (LA 55838)
SR #1365 (1986), NR #86003643 (1987), ☒ 1718

Unreachable Rockshelter (LA 55841)
SR #1368 (1986), NR #86003616 (1987), ☒ 1718

Bluewater *(Cibola County)*

Tchalchuitl Mines (LA 56755)
SR #1369 (1986)

Bloomfield *(San Juan County)*

Twin Angels Pueblo (LA 5642)
SR #689 (1978), NR #80002566 (1980), ☒ 657

Cebolleta *(Cibola County)*

Cebolleta Ruin (LA 424)
SR #95 (1969)

Los Portales
SR #69 (1969)

Church Rock Village *(McKinley County)*

Route 66: Iyanbito to Rehobeth (National Old Trails Highway)
SR #1683 (1997), NR #97001397 (1997), ☒ 1564

Coolidge *(McKinley County)*

Coolidge Archaeological District (LA 17280)
SR #679 (1978), ☒ 657

Route 66: Milan to Continental Divide
SR #1678 (1997), NR #97001394 (1997), ☒ 1564

Coyote *(San Juan County)*

Grey Hill Spring Archaeological District (LA 18244)
SR #669 (1978), ☒ 657

Coyote Canyon *(McKinley County)*

Peach Springs Archaeological District (LA 10770)
SR #665 (1978), ☒ 657

Crownpoint *(McKinley County)*

Bee Burrow Archaeological District (LA 13163)
SR #666 (1978), NR #84001296 (1984), ☒ 657

Casa de Estrella Archaeological Site (Section 8 Ruin) (LA 17225)
SR #667 (1978), NR #80002553 (1980), ☒ 657

Dalton Pass Archaeological Site (LA 98222)
SR #682 (1978), NR #80002554 (1980), ☒ 657

Greenlee Archaeological Site (LA 35418)
SR #671 (1978), NR #80002555 (1980), ☒ 657

Haystack Archaeological District (LA 6022, LA 12573)
SR #672 (1978), NR #80002556 (1980), ☒ 657

Indian Creek Archaeological District (LA 17081)
SR #677 (1978), ☒ 657

Muddy Water Archaeological District (LA 10959)
SR #675 (1978), ☒ 657

Standing Rock Archaeological District (LA 18232)
SR #681 (1978), ☒ 657

Upper Kin Klizhin Archaeological Site (LA 34245)
SR #683 (1978), NR #80002557 (1980), ☒ 657

El Morro *(Cibola County)*

Cienega Ruins (LA 425-426)
SR #96 (1969)

El Morro National Monument and Collections
NM 53
SR #59 (1969), NR #66000043 (1966)

Pueblo de los Muertos (LA 5536)
SR #109 (1969)

Farmington *(San Juan County)*

Andrews Building (Old Farmington Drug Store)
101 E. Main St.
SR #1616 (1995)

Thomas Jefferson Arrington House
506 W Arrington St.
SR #715 (1979)

Bloomfield Irrigation Ditch
SR #543 (1978)

East Side Rincon Site (LA 3131)
SR #1209 (1985), NR #85003154 (1985), ☒ 1723

Gallegos Wash Archaeological District (LA 5635)
SR #341 (1974), NR #75001165 (1975)

Hopkins Place
503 N. Auburn
SR #1591 (1994)

Jaquez Site Ruin (LA 2609)
SR #789 (1980), NR #84001281 (1984), ☒ 657

La Plata Highway Site (LA 50337)
NM 170
SR #1259 (1986), ☒ 1723

Morris Site 39 (LA 1897)
NM 170
SR #1260 (1986), ☒ 1723

Morris Site 41 Archaeological District (LA 5631)
SR #693 (1978), NR #79001548 (1979), ☒ 657

Old Indian Racetrack (LA 9050)
SR #513 (1977)

Rolling Waters Building (Old First National Bank Building)
101 W. Main St.
SR #1631 (1996)

George Salmon Homestead
975 US 64
SR #1513 (1989), SALMON RUIN ARCHAEOLOGICAL DISTRICT

Salmon Ruin (LA 8846)
SR #21 (1968), NR #70000406 (1970)

The Chacoan system, centered in the towns of Chaco Canyon in the 11th century, expanded during the years 1020-1120 to include Chacoan outliers, such as Salmon Ruin. These outlier communities may have been a response to an increasing imbalance between limited food production and a growing population. The Chacoan roads, such as the Great North Road leading from Salmon and Aztec toward Chaco Canyon, may represent an ideological or economic affiliation with the canyon. Salmon Ruin was probably founded by a local San Juan group and a Chacoan group. It is a C-shaped structure containing about 290 rooms, a great kiva and a tower kiva built in three planned episodes between 1088 and 1106. The foundations of the whole town were laid out prior to its construc-

tion, in classic Late Chacoan rubble core and banded facing masonry, on a gravel terrace facing the San Juan River. The layout shows an obvious similarity to the Classic Bonito style in Chaco Canyon. After 1107, the pueblo was modified by San Juan people; they left Salmon in the late 1200s. Salmon Ruin and a museum are open to the public.

Fort Wingate *(McKinley County)*

Fort Wingate Historic District
NM 400
SR #403 (1975), NR #78003076 (1978)

Fort Wingate Ruin (LA 2690)
SR #685 (1978), NR #80002558 (1980), ⊠ 657

Old Fort Wingate/Zuni Wagon Road
SR #163 (1970)

Fruitland *(San Juan County)*

Fruitland Trading Company (Baah Diilid)
5 CR 6677
SR #1506 (1989)

Brigham Young Jr. House
Main St.
SR #487 (1983)

LA 19305
SR #429 (1976), NR #78001823 (1978)

LA 19794
SR #430 (1976), NR #78003261 (1978)

LA 19290
SR #428 (1976), NR #78001822 (1978)

Gallup *(McKinley County)*

Atchison, Topeka & Santa Fe Railway Depot in Gallup
201 E. 66 Ave.
SR #1183 (1985), ⊠ 1724

Chief Theater
228 W. Coal Ave.
SR #1726, NR #87002223 (1988), ⊠ 1724

C.N. Cotton Warehouse
101 N. 3rd St.
SR #1179 (1985), NR #87002226 (1988), ⊠ 1724

Drake Hotel
216 E. 66 Ave.
SR #1182 (1985), NR #87002218 (1988),
☒ 1724

El Morro Theater
205-209 W. Coal Ave.
SR #1187 (1985), NR #87002221 (1988),
☒ 1724

El Rancho Hotel
1000 E. 66 Ave.
SR #1190 (1985), NR #87002222 (1988),
☒ 1724

The motion picture industry arrived in Gallup in the early 1900s to take advantage of the town's picturesque high desert setting. R.E. "Griff" Griffith, brother of pioneering movie director D.W. Griffith, came to Gallup in the early 1930s to make a movie, and returned to build El Rancho Hotel in 1936. The hotel is a three-story Rustic Style building built of brick, random ashlar stone and rough-hewn wood, with brick and stone chimneys and a pitched wood shake roof. Some brickwork exhibits an unusual wavy pattern that emphasizes the hotel's rustic appearance. The two-story lobby, with its criss-cross balustrade balcony, suggests a hunting lodge. At the rear of the lobby is an impressive walk-in fireplace cove of brick and random ashlar. The wooden stairways are made of split logs. El Rancho Hotel is associated not only with the motion picture industry, but also with the tourist trade brought by historic Route 66. It continues to operate as a hotel.

Grand Hotel (Ricca's Mercantile)
306 W. Coal Ave.
SR #1184 (1985), NR #87002217 (1988),
☒ 1724

Harrison House
202 E. Hill St.
SR #537 (1977)

Harvey Hotel
408 W. Coal Ave.
SR #1185 (1985), NR #87002219 (1988),
☒ 1724

LA 38011
SR #889 (1982)

Lebanon Lodge No. 22
106 W. Aztec
SR #1188 (1985), NR #87002225 (1989),
☒ 1724

Log Cabin Motel
1010 W. 66 Ave.
SR #1580 (1993), NR #93001213 (1993),
☒ 1564

McKinley County Courthouse
205-209 W. Hill St.
SR #1191 (1985), NR #87000879 (1989),
☒ 1724, ☒ 1722

Mentmore Meadows Archaeological Site
SR #1376 (1987)

Old U.S. Post Office (Clay Fultz Agency)
201 S. 1st St.
SR #1189 (1985), NR #87002228 (1988), ⊠ 1724

Palace Hotel
236 W. 66 Ave.
SR #1181 (1985), NR #87002216 (1988), ⊠ 1724

Peggy's Pueblo (LA 76000)
SR #1592 (1994), NR #94000993 (1994), ⊠ 657

Redwood Lodge (Jim's Modern Court)
907 E. 66 Ave.
SR #1685 (1997), NR #98000051 (1998), ⊠ 1564

Rex Hotel
300 W. 66 Ave.
SR #1180 (1985), NR #87002215 (1988), ⊠ 1724

White Cafe
100 W. 66 Ave.
SR #1186 (1985), NR #87002212 (1988), ⊠ 1724

Gamerco *(McKinley County)*

Gamerco Mine Smokestack
Highway 666
SR #492 (1977)

Grants *(Cibola County)*

Jesus Blea House
543 Valencia Rd.
SR #750 (1979)

Candelaria Pueblo (Las Ventanas Site) (LA 1328)
SR #847 (1981), NR #83001619 (1983), ⊠ 657

Dittert Site (LA 11723)
SR #444 (1976), NR #77000931 (1977)

Route 66: McCartys to Grants
SR #1677 (1997), NR #97001398 (1997), ⊠ 1564

Laguna *(Cibola County)*

SEE ALSO CENTRAL REGION

Correo Snake Pit and Collections
SR #436 (1976)

Encinal Day School
SR #767 (1980), NR #80002576 (1980)

Masonry Dam of the Rio Puerco
SR #226 (1971)

Pueblo of Laguna
SR #228 (1971), NR #73001154 (1973)

San Jose de la Laguna Mission Church and Convento
SR #233 (1971), NR #73001155 (1973), PUEBLO OF LAGUNA DISTRICT

La Plata *(San Juan County)*

Holmes Group (LA 1898)
NM 170
SR #66 (1986), ⊠ 1723

Ridge Site (LA 37972)
SR #1258 (1986), ⊠ 1723

Manuelito *(McKinley County)*

Atsee Nitsaa (LA 1507, LA 47588-47591)
SR #1291 (1986), ⊠ 1721

Big House (LA 1379)

SR #1294 (1986), ⊠ 1721

Kin Hocho'i (LA 6541)

SR #1290 (1986), ⊠ 1721

Manuelito Complex (LA 2341) ▲

SR #239 (1972), NR #66000894 (1966)

Manuelito Canyon is a broad sandy floodplain, cut by a narrow deep arroyo, running northwest from a high divide to a confluence with the Puerco River. To the east of the floodplain is a massive ridge cut by tributary canyons; to the west is a vertical sandstone cliff forming the edge of a mesa in which numerous tributaries create sheer walled alcoves and rincons deep in the mesa's flank. The canyon was continuously occupied from about A.D. 700 to about 1350 by Anasazi people. Beginning around 1000, sites became larger, with pueblos consisting of blocks of contiguous masonry rooms, usually fewer than ten rooms at first, then with 20 to 25 rooms or more. One large site called *Kin Hoho'i* located near the confluence of Manuelito Canyon and the Puerco River is a Chacoan outlier with two great kivas. This site was occupied between 1050 and 1150, then replaced as the major site in Manuelito by *Atsee Nitsaa,* another large site with a great kiva. Occupied from the mid 1100s through the early 1200s, this site was in turn replaced as the major center of the Manuelito Complex by the very large Big House pueblo, which was occupied until the early 1300s. The canyon was virtually unoccupied from about 1350 until 1700, when Navajo people moved into the area. Manuelito Canyon contains an enormously rich and complex record of American Indian culture history, preserving 700 years of continuous Anasazi occupation, intermittent use by Zuni people for about 500 years, and 200 years of Navajo occupation.

Naat'a'anii Bikin, Tower Ruin (LA 1502)

SR #1295 (1986), ⊠ 1721

Stepping Stone House (LA 2340)

SR #1292 (1986), ⊠ 1721

Wolye A'din (LA 47505)

SR #1293 (1986), ⊠ 1721

Mentmore *(McKinley County)*

Route 66: Manuelito to the Arizona Border

SR #1581 (1993), NR #93001209 (1993), ⊠ 1564

Chaco Canyon – Nageezi *(San Juan County)*

Bisa'ani Archaeological District (LA 17287)

SR #684 (1978), ⊠ 657

Chaco Culture National Historical Park ◎

SR #57 (1969), NR #66000895 (1966)

Chaco Canyon is 20 miles long and one-half to three-quarters of a mile wide. Although there are no living streams in

Chaco Canyon, it is relatively well watered, not by precipitation but by runoff that pours from the cliffs into the canyon during storms, and by numerous tributaries to the Chaco Wash that drain large areas of the surrounding San Juan Basin. By about A.D. 500, there were pithouse settlements on the mesa tops above the canyon and in the rolling hills to the south. People began to use the canyon bottomlands extensively around A.D. 750, and around 850 the first communities developed. These included both small, largely domestic villages and "great houses," large, elaborate buildings with more public functions. The complex at Chaco Canyon is renowned for its spectacular great kivas, imaginative cut stone architecture, and pictographs and petroglyphs including the "sun dagger" archaeoastronomy site. The Chacoan system expanded during the years from 1020 to 1120 to include outlier communities throughout the San Juan Basin and beyond, a vast area about the size of England. Many of the outlier sites were connected to each other and to Chaco Canyon by straight, carefully designed roads, and Chaco Canyon became the center of a trade network extending into Mexico. The last addition to a canyon great house was completed in 1132. By 1150, the great houses were largely abandoned, probably due to a series of droughts that caused the agricultural and social systems to fail.

Lake Valley Archaeological Site (LA 18755)

SR #668 (1978), ☒ 657

Romulo Martinez Trading Post Site (LA 87860-87861)

CR 7575

SR #1544 (1992)

Whirlwind Lake Archaeological District (LA18237)

SR #674 (1978), ☒ 657

Ojo Caliente *(Cibola County)*

SEE ALSO NORTH-CENTRAL REGION

Hinkson Ranch Pueblo (LA 11439)

SR #1296 (1986), ☒ 1721

Jalarosa Pueblo (LA 3993)

SR #1298 (1986), ☒ 1721

Ojo Bonito Pueblo (LA 11433)

SR #1297 (1986), ☒ 1721

Prewitt *(McKinley County)*

Andrews Archaeological District (LA 17218)

SR #691 (1978), NR #79003129 (1979), ☒ 657

Casa Mero Archaeological District (LA 8779)

SR #688 (1978), ☒ 657

Casa Mero (Casamero) Ruin (LA 8779)

SR #423 (1975), CASA MERO ARCHAEOLOGICAL DISTRICT, ⊠ 657

Coyotes Sing Here Archaeological District (LA 18754)

SR #680 (1978), ⊠ 657

Pueblo Pintado *(McKinley County)*

Chaco Mesa Pueblo III

MULTIPLE PROPERTY LISTING

⊠ 1725

Found on the piñon and juniper dotted ridges along Chaco Mesa, the forty archaeological sites included in this multiple property listing represent one of the best-preserved examples of post-Chacoan, Pueblo III Anazazi settlements in the San Juan Basin. Occupied between 1175 and 1275, individual sites in this thematic group include villages of 50 to 75 rooms, small residences of one or two rooms, several large isolated pit depressions, and three prehistoric road segments. The village sites are remarkably similar in size, layout and construction. They are visible today as mounds of rubble, often arranged around plazas, and are associated with pit structures or kivas, middens, and diffuse scatters of pottery and stone tools. Chaco Mesa Pueblo III sites include:

LA 45780, SR #1163 (1985), NR #85001701 (1985), ⊠ 1725; **LA 45781,** SR #1164 (1985), NR #85001702 (1985), ⊠ 1725; **LA 45782,** SR #1165 (1985), NR #85001703 (1985), ⊠ 1725; **LA 45784,** SR #1166 (1985), NR #85001704 (1985), ⊠ 1725, **LA 45785** SR #1167 (1985), NR #85001705 (1985), ⊠ 1725; **LA 45786** SR #1168 (1985), NR #85001706 (1985), ⊠ 1725; **LA 45789,** SR #1169 (1985), NR #85001707 (1985), ⊠ 1725, **LA 50000,** SR #1130 (1985), NR #85001708 (1985), ⊠ 1725; **LA 50001,** SR #1131 (1985), NR #85001709 (1985), ⊠ 1725; **LA 50013,** SR #1133 (1985), NR #85001710 (1985), ⊠ 1725; **LA 50014,** SR #1134 (1985), NR #85001711 (1985), ⊠ 1725; **LA 50015,** SR #1135 (1985), NR #85001712 (1985), ⊠ 1725; **LA 50016,** SR #1136 (1985), NR #85001713 (1985), ⊠ 1725; **LA 50017,** SR #1137 (1985), NR #85001714 (1985), ⊠ 1725; **LA 50018,** SR #1138 (1985), NR #85001715 (1985), ⊠ 1725; **LA 50019,** SR #1139 (1985), NR #85001716 (1985), ⊠ 1725; **LA 50020,** SR #1140 (1985), NR #85001717 (1985), ⊠ 1725; **LA 50021,** SR #1141 (1985), NR #85001718 (1985), ⊠ 1725; **LA 50022,** SR #1142 (1985), NR #85001719 (1985), ⊠ 1725; **LA 50023,** SR #1143 (1985), NR #85001720 (1985), ⊠ 1725; **LA 50024,** SR #1144 (1985), NR #85001721 (1985), ⊠ 1725; **LA 50025,** SR #1145 (1985), NR #85001722 (1985), ⊠ 1725; **LA 50026,** SR #1146 (1985), NR #85001723 (1985), ⊠ 1725; **LA 50027,** SR #1147 (1985), NR #85001724 (1985), ⊠ 1725; **LA 50028** SR #1148 (1985), NR #85001725 (1985), ⊠ 1725; **LA 50030,** SR #1149 (1985), NR #85001726 (1985), ⊠ 1725; **LA 50031,** SR #1150 (1985), NR #85001727 (1985), ⊠ 1725; **LA 50033,** SR #1151 (1985), NR #85001728 (1985), ⊠ 1725;

LA 50034 SR #1152 (1985), NR #85001729 (1985), ⊠ 1725; **LA 50035,** SR #1153 (1985), NR #85001743 (1985), ⊠ 1725; **LA 50036,** SR #1154 (1985), NR #85001730 (1985), ⊠ 1725; **LA 50037,** SR #1155 (1985), NR #85001731 (1985), ⊠ 1725; **LA 50038,** SR #1156 (1985), NR #85001732 (1985), ⊠ 1725; **LA 50044,** SR #1157 (1985), NR #85001733 (1985), ⊠ 1725; **LA 50071,** SR #1158 (1985), NR #85001734 (1985), ⊠ 1725; **LA 50072,** SR #1159 (1985), NR #85001735 (1985), ⊠ 1725; **LA 50074,** SR #1160 (1985), NR #85001736 (1985), ⊠ 1725; **LA 50077,** SR #1161 (1985), NR #85001737 (1985), ⊠ 1725; **LA 50080,** SR #1162 (1985), NR #85001738 (1985), ⊠ 1725; **Reservoir Site (LA 15278),** SR #1132 (1985), NR #85001700 (1985), ⊠ 1725

Ramah *(McKinley County)*

Ashcroft/Merrill Historic District (Shady Haven)
Bloomfield St. and McNeil
SR #1374 (1987), NR #90001079 (1990)

Joseph Alright Boot Bond House (Maggie Bond House)
Bloomfield St. and Lewis St.
SR 1609 (1995)

Gigantes Ruin (LA 1551)
SR #102 (1969)

Evon Zartman Vogt Ranch House
NM 53
SR #1509 (1989), NR #92001819 (1993)

Red Hill *(Cibola County)*

Fort Atarque Ruin (LA 55367)
SR #1300 (1986), ⊠ 1721

San Fidel *(Cibola County)*

Route 66: Laguna to McCarty's
SR #1589 (1993), NR #93001466 (1994), ⊠ 1564

St. Joseph School
NM 124
SR #1561 (1993)

San Mateo *(Cibola County)*

San Mateo Archaeological Site (LA 15369)
SR #692 (1978), NR #79001563 (1979), ⊠ 657

Kin Nizhoni (LA 18166)
NM 53 and NM 509
SR #687 (1978), ⊠ 657

Sheep Springs *(San Juan County)*

Great Bend Community Archaeological District (LA 6419)
SR #676 (1978), ⊠ 657

Willow Canyon Archaeological District (LA 18235)
SR #678 (1978), ⊠ 657

Shiprock *(San Juan County)*

Hogback Archaeological District (LA 11207, LA 11594)
SR #670 (1978), ⊠ 657

Hogback Ruin (LA 11594)
SR #250 (1972), HOGBACK ARCHAEOLOGICAL DISTRICT, ⊠ 657

Mitten Rock Archaeological District (LA 8243)

SR #251 (1971)

Pictured Cliffs Archaeological Site (LA 8970)

NM 550

SR #105 (1969)

San Juan River Bridge

US 666

SR #575 (1978)

San Juan River Bridge at Shiprock

US 666

SR #1666 (1997), NR #97000740 (1997), ☒ 1661

Thoreau *(McKinley County)*

Roy T. Herman's Garage and Service Station

NM 122, west of I-40 exit

SR #1579 (1993), NR #93001212 (1993), ☒ 1564

Toadlena *(San Juan County)*

Crumbled House Archaeological District (LA 7070)

SR #98 (1969), ☒ 657

Skunk Springs Archaeological District (LA 7000)

SR #120 (1969), ☒ 657

Skunk Springs/Crumbled House Archaeological District (LA 7000)

SR #673 (1969), ☒ 657

Two Grey Hills Archaeological District (LA 7979, LA 7000, LA 7007, LA 7070, LA 7080)

SR #31 (1968)

Two Grey Hills Trading Post (LA 114751)

SR #1514 (1989)

Yellow Adobe Site (LA 7979)

SR #127 (1969)

Tohatchi *(McKinley County)*

Tohatchi Village Site (LA 3098)

SR #123 (1969)

Zuni Pueblo *(McKinley County)*

Hawikuh Ruin (LA 37) ▲

(in Cibola County)

SR #10 (1968), NR #66000502 (1966)

The Zuni community of Hawikuh, which may have been founded in the 1300s, developed into a multistoried adobe pueblo. It was the largest of the six Zuni towns when the Spanish first visited the area in 1539. After seeing the desert sunlight on the adobe buildings from a distance, the first explorers returned to New Spain (Mexico) and told a tale of a golden city called Cibola. This inspired explorer Francisco Vasquez Coronado's search for the seven cities of Cibola. In 1540, he engaged in a fierce battle here, inflicting heavy casualties on the Zunis. The first Catholic mission to the Zuni people began at Hawikuh in 1629. In the Pueblo Revolt of 1680, the mission was destroyed, and the people fled to the mesas. They returned in 1692 to the single town of Zuni (Halona), leaving Hawikuh and the other towns empty.

Heshotauthla Ruin (LA 2114)

SR #103 (1969), ZUNI-CIBOLA COMPLEX ARCHAEOLOGICAL DISTRICT

Kechiba:wa Ruin (LA 8758)
(in Cibola County)
SR #285 (1973), ZUNI-CIBOLA COMPLEX ARCHAEOLOGICAL DISTRICT

Kyaki:ma Ruin (LA 492)
SR #286 (1973), ZUNI-CIBOLA COMPLEX ARCHAEOLOGICAL DISTRICT

Kwa'kin'a Ruin (LA 1053)
SR #287 (6-20-73), ZUNI-CIBOLA COMPLEX ARCHAEOLOGICAL DISTRICT

Mats'a:kya Ruin (LA 27713)
SR #288 (1973), ZUNI-CIBOLA COMPLEX ARCHAEOLOGICAL DISTRICT

Ojo Pueblo (LA 27612)
(in Cibola County)
SR #797 (1982)

Soldado Ruin (LA 433)
SR #121 (1969)

Tucson Gas and Electric Route Sites (14 Sites) *(in Cibola County)*
SR #263 (1972)

Village of the Great Kivas (LA 631)
SR #290 (1973), ZUNI-CIBOLA COMPLEX ARCHAEOLOGICAL DISTRICT

Yellow House Ruin (LA 493)
SR #128 (1969), ZUNI-CIBOLA COMPLEX ARCHAEOLOGICAL DISTRICT

Zuni-Cibola Complex ▲
(in McKinley and Cibola Counties)
SR #374 (1975), NR #74002267 (1974)

The Zuni-Cibola Complex actually consists of four separate, non-contiguous sites: the Village of the Great Kivas, Yellow House, Kechiba:wa and Hawikuh. Together they illustrate the development of Zuni culture and its continuity from prehistoric times to the present day. The Village of the Great Kivas, with two great kivas and three roomblocks, is located at the mouth of Red Paint Canyon. It was built in the A.D. 1000s and occupied through the 1200s. Yellow House, on a low ridge north of Pescado Creek, was mainly occupied in the 1300s. It has never been excavated, but may have as many as 250 rooms and several kivas. Hawikuh may have been founded in the 1300s; it developed into a large multi-storied pueblo occupied until after Spanish contact in 1540. Kechiba:wa is located on a sandstone escarpment about three miles east of Hawikuh, and was occupied about the same time. It is a pueblo of 150 to 200 rooms and at least two plazas. When the Spanish arrived in 1539 searching for mineral resources, the Zuni were the first native people of the American Southwest to encounter Europeans. The descendants of the occupants of these villages still live in the same region today.

Zuni Dam
SR #582 (1978)

Zuni Mission Church, Restored
SR #169 (1970), ZUNI-CIBOLA COMPLEX ARCHAEOLOGICAL DISTRICT

Zuni Pueblo (Halona Pueblo)
SR #255 (1972), NR #75002066 (1975)

North-Central

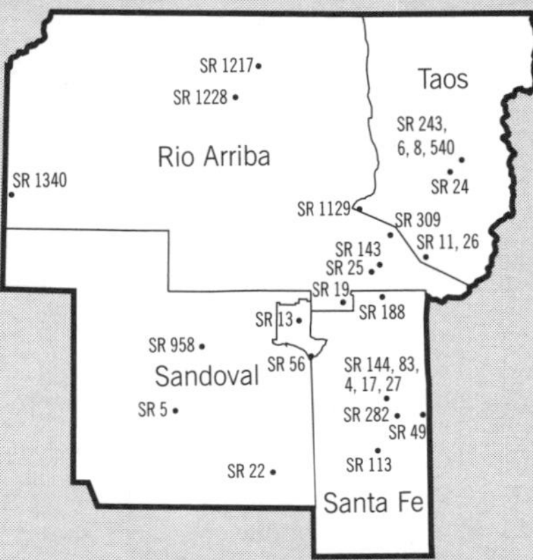

The North-Central region of New Mexico is dominated by high mountain ranges with their forests of aspen and conifers and by the valleys of the Rio Grande and the Chama River. The Sangre de Cristo, San Juan and Jemez mountains and the permanent water sources have shaped life in this region for thousands of years. This region was home to large numbers of late prehistoric Pueblo people and to their modern descendants at Taos, Jemez and the northern and middle Rio Grande pueblos. It is also the homeland of the Jicarilla Apache people, and for the past 400 years has been the heartland of Hispanic settlement and culture in New Mexico. The State and National Register listings in north-central New Mexico are dominated by the Hispanic and Pueblo cultures—large prehistoric pueblos, historic pueblos, Spanish colonial and territorial era villages, land grants, and adobe churches—places which reflect the beauty of this dramatic landscape. Also reflected in the register listing are such disparate themes as the artistic communities of Santa Fe and Taos, the Cold War significance of Los Alamos, the history of New Mexico territorial and state government, and those workhorses of commerce in 19th and early 20th century New Mexico, the narrow-gauge railroads.

Abiquiu *(Rio Arriba County)*

Abiquiu Mesa Grid Gardens (Abiquiu Archaeological District) (LA 275, LA 4934)
SR #859 (1982), NR #82001051 (1982),
☒ 1703

Abiquiu Canyon Archaeological District (LA 55882)
SR #1397 (1987), ☒ 1703

Cerrito Recreation Site, Abiquiu Reservoir
SR #402 (1975)

Cerro Colorado Archaeological District (LA 307)
NM 96
SR #1399 (1987), ☒ 1703

Christ-in-the-Desert Monastery
SR #134 (1969)

East Morada at Abiquiu
South of US 84
SR #196 (1970)

Tomás Gonzales House (Mormon House)
CR 155, east of junction with US 84
SR #1629 (1996), NR #96000258 (1996)

Leafwater Archaeological District (LA 300, LA 918)
SR #928 (1983), NR #83004155 (1983),
☒ 1703

Palisade Archaeological District (LA 3505)
NM 96
SR #1396 (1987), ☒ 1703

Plaza Blanca Community Ditch
From Chama River
SR #1227 (1986), NR #86002298 (1986),
☒ 1705

Plaza Blanca Historic District
Along Plaza Blanca Rd. to Old La Puente Ford Rd.
SR #1215 (1986), NR #86002322 (1986), ⊠ 1705

Poshuinge Archaeological District (LA 274)
SR #1398 (1987), NR #93000675 (1993), ⊠ 1703

Santa Rosa de Lima de Abiquiu
SR #118 (1969), NR #78001820 (1978)

Tsama Archaeological District (LA 908-909)
SR #929 (1983), NR #83004158 (1983), ⊠ 1703

Alcalde *(Rio Arriba County)*

La Capilla de San Francisco de Asís
NM 582 in Estaca
SR #1640 (1996)

Los Luceros Hacienda
SR #143 (1970), NR #83004157 (1983)

Los Luceros, in a floodplain about 300 yards from the Rio Grande in the middle of a commercial apple orchard, is a historic ranch or *hacienda* that includes five historic structures: a two-story double-galleried house with Greek Revival style decorative detailing; a Late Victorian cottage; a chapel, Capilla de Nuestra Señora de Guadalupe; a flat-roofed adobe structure said to have been used at one time as a jail; and an adobe guest house. The main house probably incorporates parts of the 18th century rancho of Captain Sebastián Martín Serrano, a leader of the Reconquest, and may be on a prehistoric site as well (evidenced by ceramics dating from around the 15th century). It was remodeled in the 1850s in Greek Revival style by Elias T. Clark, a Missouri trader. The house plan, with rooms flanking a central hall on both floors, is a Greek Revival innovation of the Territorial period. Mary Cabot Wheelwright, art collector and founder of Santa Fe's Wheelwright Museum, acquired Los Luceros in the 1920s and carried out some Pueblo Revival style remodeling of the main house, "jail" and guest house. The historic ranch complex is one of the most complete haciendas in northern New Mexico from the period in the 19th century when New Mexico was a territory of the United States. Various changes of ownership in the last twenty years have left the buildings in a state of disrepair.

San Antonio de Padua Morada
Alcalde Plaza
SR #352 (1974)

Algodones *(Sandoval County)*

Espinosa Ridge Pueblo (LA 278)
SR #913 (1983), NR #84003012 (1984)

Pueblo Tuerto (LA 38928)
SR #912 (1983), NR #84003042 (1984)

Tonque Pueblo (LA 240)
SR #915 (1983), NR #84003045 (1984)

Arroyo Hondo *(Taos County)*

Turley Mill and Distillery Site
SR #416 (1975), NR #78001833 (1978)

Arroyo Seco *(Taos County)*

San Ignacio de Loyola Morada
503 Arroyo Hondo/Seco Rd.
SR #1657 (1997)

Bernalillo *(Sandoval County)*

Coronado State Monument and Visitor Center
North of NM 44
SR #1515 (1989), KUAUA RUINS ARCHAEOLOGICAL DISTRICT

Kuaua Ruins (LA 187)
Coronado State Monument
SR #225 (1971), NR #76001199 (1976)

Las Cocinitas
Original plaza of Bernalillo, bounded by Avenida Bernalillo, Calle San Felipe, Calle San Lorenzo and Calle Don Francisco
SR #37 (1969)

Our Lady of Sorrows Church
281 Camino del Pueblo
SR #164 (1970), NR #77000927 (1977)

Our Lady of Sorrows Convent
264 Camino del Pueblo
SR #709 (1978)

Pueblo Santiago (LA 326, LA 728)
SR #1247 (1986), ☒ 1720

Roosevelt School
Calle Malinche
SR #1619 (1996), NR #96000266 (1996), ☒ 1617

Abenicio Salazar Historic District
282 Camino del Pueblo
SR #743 (1979), NR #80002569 (1980)

Spanish Entrada Site (LA 54147)
NM 528
SR #1382 (1987)

Blanco *(Rio Arriba County)*

SEE ALSO NORTHWEST REGION

Adams Canyon Site (LA 55824)
SR #1351 (1986), NR #86003631 (1987), ☒ 1718

Adolfo Canyon Site (LA 5665)
SR #1341 (1986), NR #86003605 (1987), ☒ 1718

Boulder Fortress (LA 55828)
SR #1352 (1986), NR #86003630 (1987), ☒ 1718

Cabresto Mesa Tower Complex (LA 2138)
SR #1332 (1986), NR #86003611 (1987), ☒ 1718

Cagle's Site (LA 55826)
SR #1353 (1986), NR #86003629 (1987), ☒ 1718

Canyon View Ruin (LA 55827)
SR #1354 (1986), NR #86003628 (1987), ☒ 1718

Casa Mesa Diablo (LA 11100)
SR #1346 (1986), NR #86003641 (1987), ☒ 1718

The Citadel (LA 55828)
SR #1355 (1986), NR #86003627 (1987), CROW CANYON ARCHAEOLOGICAL DISTRICT, ☒ 1718

Compressor Station Ruin (LA 5658)
SR #1337 (1986), NR #86003592 (1987), ☒ 1718

Crevice Ruin (LA 13218)
SR #1348 (1986), NR #86003639 (1987), ☒ 1718

Crow Canyon Archaeological District (LA 20219)
SR #276 (1973), NR #74001200 (1974)

Crow Canyon Site (LA 20219)
SR #1349 (1986), NR #86003638 (1987), CROW CANYON ARCHAEOLOGICAL DISTRICT, 1718

Delgadito Pueblito (LA 5649)
SR #1336 (1986), NR #86003590 (1987), ☒ 1718

Foothold Ruin (LA 9073)
SR #1343 (1986), NR #86003602 (1987), ☒ 1718

Frances Canyon Ruin (LA 2135, LA 9072)
SR #100 (1969), NR #70000404 (1970), NR #87000244 (1987), ☒ 1718

García Canyon Pueblito (LA 36608)
SR #1350 (1986), NR #86003636 (1987), ☒ 1718

Gomez Canyon Ruin (LA 55831)
SR #1358 (1986), NR #86003626 (1987), ☒ 1718

Gomez Point Site (LA 58832)
SR #1359 (1986), NR #86003625 (1987), ☒ 1718

Gould Pass Ruin (LA 5659)
SR #1338 (1986), NR #86003594 (1987), ☒ 1718

Hill Road Ruin (LA 55833)
SR #1360 (1986), NR #86003624 (1987), ☒ 1718

Hooded Fireplace Ruin (LA 5662)
SR #364 (1975), NR #86003607 (1987), ☒ 1718

Kin Naa daa' (Maize House) (LA 1872)
SR #1331 (1986), NR #86003612 (1987), ☒ 1718

Kin Yazhi (Little House) (LA 2433)
SR #1333 (1986), NR #86003609 (1987), ☒ 1718

Largo School Ruin (LA 5657)
SR #365 (1975), NR #86003621 (1987), ☒ 1718

Old Fort Ruin (LA 1869)
SR #15 (1968), NR #86003614 (1987), ☒ 1718

Overlook Site (LA 10732)
SR #1344 (1986), NR #86003601 (1987), ☒ 1718

Pointed Butte Ruin (LA 10733)
SR #1345 (1986), NR #86003600 (1987), ☒ 1718

Pork Chop Pass Site (LA 5661)
SR #1340 (1986), NR #86003597 (1987), ☒ 1718

The Pork Chop Pass Site sits high on the mesa west of the junction of Largo and Palluche Canyons. The site was probably occupied from about 1725 to about 1750 by Navajo people. This area is called the *Dinetah* and is considered by the Navajo to be their original homeland. Pork Chop Pass Site consists of a *pueblito,* a term often used for the small defensive pueblos of this area and period, and a separate masonry structure. The *pueblito* has three ground floor rooms and a passageway connecting two of the rooms. It has narrow doorways, columnar masonry, north and east facing doors and beams cut with a metal axe.

These features are common to other nearby 18th century sites, but Pork Chop Pass differs in its combination of rectangular and oval rooms.

Pueblito Canyon Ruin (LA 1684)
SR #1330 (1986), NR #86003615 (1987), ⊠ 1718

Pueblito East Ruin (LA 55834)
SR #1361 (1986), NR #86003623 (1987), ⊠ 1718

Ridge Top House (LA 6287)
SR #1342 (1986), NR #86003603 (1987), CROW CANYON ARCHAEOLOGICAL DISTRICT, ⊠ 1718

Rincon Largo Ruin (LA 2435, LA 2436)
SR #1335 (1986), NR #86003589 (1987), ⊠ 1718

Rincon Rockshelter (LA 55835)
SR #1362 (1986), NR #86003622 (1987), ⊠ 1718

Romine Canyon Ruin (LA 55836)
SR #1363 (1986), NR #86003620 (1987), ⊠ 1718

Romine Ranch Ruin (LA 55837)
SR #1364 (1986), NR #86003619 (1987), ⊠ 1718

Shaft House (LA 5660)
SR #1339 (1986), NR #86003595 (1987), CROW CANYON ARCHAEOLOGICAL DISTRICT, ⊠ 1718

Split Rock Ruin (LA 5664)
SR #372 (1975), NR #86003606 (1987), ⊠ 1718

Tapicito Ruin (LA 2298)
SR #262 (1972), NR #86003610 (1987), ⊠ 1718

Three Corn Ruin (LA 1871)
SR #29 (1968), NR #86003613 (1987), ⊠ 1718

Tower of the Standing God (LA 55839)
SR #1366 (1986), NR #86003618 (1987), ⊠ 1718

Truby's Tower (LA 2434)
SR #1334 (1986), NR #86003608 (1987), ⊠ 1718

The Wall (LA 55840)
SR #1367 (1986), NR #86003617 (1987), ⊠ 1718

Brazos *(Rio Arriba County)*

El Barranco Community Ditch
From the Chama River to Upper Brazos Ditch
SR #1228 (1986), NR #86002296 (1986), ⊠ 1705

The village of Los Brazos and the nearby villages of Los Ojos, La Puente, Tierra Amarilla and Plaza Blanca are among the least-altered 19th century Hispanic New Mexican communities. The network of seven irrigation systems serving these villages was and is vital to the local government and economy. The ditches, called *acequias,* irrigate fields that produce grasses and grains including alfalfa, timothy and barley. The *acequias* are owned and managed by their users, called *parciantes,* and originate at higher elevations at concrete headgates on the Rio Brazos, Rito de Tierra Amarilla and Rio Chama. The *acequias* were dug, using crude hand implements and ox-drawn plows, shortly after the Tierra Amarilla Land Grant allowed

permanent settlement. The *acequias* were planned so that all possessing land would have access to water, and the fields were laid out with a slight slope to ensure complete water coverage. El Barranco, built in 1907, is one of the later ditches in the system. Despite the loss of common lands to Anglo speculators, the advent of a cash economy, and the exodus of many young people from the area, many of the historic structures of the area, including its ditch systems, remain in use today.

Los Brazos Historic District
Bounded by US 84, North Rd., east fence line and Rio Brazos
SR #1114 (1985), NR #85000827 (1985), ☒ 1705

Samuel Sanchez Barns
North of US 84 and NM 162
SR #1218 (1986), NR #86002317 (1986), ☒ 1705

Samuel Sanchez House
North of US 84 and NM 162
SR #1219 (1986), NR #86002315 (1986), ☒ 1705

Canjilon *(Rio Arriba County)*

Canjilon Mountain Lookout Cabin
SR #1437 (1988), ☒ 1708

Turkey Springs Archaeological Site (Turkey Springs 2) (LA 10641, LA 10642, LA 10643)
SR #275 (1973)

Cañoncito *(Santa Fe County)*

Nuestra Senora de Luz Church and Cemetery
I-25 Frontage Rd.
SR #1256 (1986), NR #95001452 (1995), ☒ 1615

Cebolla *(Rio Arriba County)*

Red Hill Archaeological Sites (LA 10644)
SR #274 (1973)

Victor Ortega Cabin
Carson National Forest
SR #1732, NR #87002456 (1988), ☒ 1708

Cebolleta *(Cibola County)*

Cañon de Juan Tafoya
(in Sandoval County)
NM 279, Marquez
SR #440 (1976)

Chama *(Rio Arriba County)*

Burns/Kelly Store
Terrace Ave. and 5th St.
SR #1253 (1986)

Chama Jail House
SR #382 (1975)

Cumbres and Toltec Scenic Railroad
64 miles between Chama and Antonito, CO
SR #136 (1969), NR #73000462 (1974)

Dunham Log House (Palmer/Dunham House)
4th St. and Maple St.
SR #1501 (1989)

Foster Hotel (Chama Hotel)
4th St. and Terrace St.
SR #357 (1975), NR #86000225 (1986)

Chimayó *(Santa Fe County)*

El Santuario de Chimayó and Collections ▲
Northwest of Santa Cruz Reservoir Dam
SR #188 (1970), NR #70000412 (1970)

Originally a private chapel, now owned by the Archdiocese of Santa Fe, the Santuario de Nuestro Señor de Esquipulas, known as El Santuario de Chimayó, is a small adobe chapel with twin bell towers and a single-aisle nave leading to a trapezoidal sanctuary. Built at the end of the colonial period, the Santuario is an example of the Spanish Colonial churches established by the Franciscan missionaries of the 17th century and modified in northern New Mexico vernacular tradition. It was built by Bernard Abeyta between 1814 and 1816; the only major modification was a pitched metal roof added in the 1920s. The sacristy is filled with devotional objects, many donated by the faithful, and hung with the crutches of devotees who have prayed for cures. Another small room holds "El Posito," a hole in the floor filled with earth believed to possess healing powers. The Santuario also contains a unique collection of Spanish Colonial religious art including wooden *retablos* (screens) and *bultos* (statues). The chapel was built to venerate Nuestro Señor de Esquipulas (a manifestation of the crucified Christ), originally worshipped in Guatemala as a source of healing through geophagy, the ingestion of sacred, curative earth. The devotional cult of Santo Niño de Atocha, now evident in the Santuario, was introduced to Chimayó about 1857. Pilgrims still walk to the Santuario every year during Holy Week from all across New Mexico and beyond to pray for cures.

Oratorio de San Buenaventura
Plaza del Cerro
SR #71 (1969), PLAZA DEL CERRO DISTRICT

Plaza del Cerro
NM 76 and 4
SR #75 (1969), NR #72000810 (1972)

Santa Cruz Dam
SR #576 (1978)

Jose Raphael Trujillo House
NM 4, Rio Chiquito
SR #1490 (1988)

Cordova *(Rio Arriba County)*

San Antonio de Padua del Quemado Chapel
NM 76
SR #369 (1975), NR #78001821 (1978)

Trujillo Mill
SR #358 (1975)

Corrales *(Sandoval County)*

Casa San Ysidro and Collections
North side of Corrales Plaza
SR #698 (1978)

Alehandro Gonzales House
4499 Corrales Rd.
SR #1516 (1989)

Pueblo Corrales (LA 288, LA 1844)
NM 46
SR #1245 (1986), ☒ 1720

San Ysidro Church
Old Church Rd.
SR #726 (1979), NR #80002570 (1980)

Coyote *(Rio Arriba County)*

Alcove Site (LA 24807)
SR #1764, NR #93001421 (1993), ☒ 1751

Rio Chama Site (LA 25473)
SR #1765, NR #93001424 (1993), ☒ 1751

Cundiyo *(Santa Fe County)*

Cundiyo
Junction of Santa Cruz and Frijoles Rivers
SR #195 (1970)

Dixon *(Taos County)*

Harding Mine
Off NM 75
SR #553 (1978)

Domingo *(Sandoval County)*

Santo Domingo Indian Trading Post
Intersection of Route 66 and
railroad tracks
SR #1684 (1997), NR #97001592 (1998),
☒ 1564

Dulce *(Rio Arriba County)*

Jicarilla Apache Historic District
Main St., NM 17, Apache Dr.,
Keliiaa Dr., and Sand Hill Dr.
SR #983 (1983), NR #84002956 (1984)

La Jara Site (Vicenti Site) (LA 14318)
SR #532 (1977), NR #79001546 (1979)

El Rito *(Rio Arriba County)*

Delgado Hall (NNMCC)
NM 96
SR #1257 (1986)

Sapawe Archaeological District (LA 306)
NM 96
SR #1400 (1987), ☒ 1703

Embudo *(Rio Arriba County)*

Embudo Historic District
NM 68
SR #485 (1977), NR #79001547 (1979)

Embudo Gauging Station
SR #309 (1974), EMBUDO HISTORIC DISTRICT

The name Embudo, meaning funnel, was given to the narrow canyon of the fast-flowing Rio Grande by Spanish settlers in the 17th century. Embudo was selected for the location of the first stream gauging station established by the U.S. Geological Survey because of its location in an arid region on a swift river unlikely to freeze in winter. The station was built in 1888, one thousand feet southeast of the Denver and Rio Grande's Embudo railroad depot, to collect data on the flow of the Rio Grande and to serve as a training area for a group of young engineers who would go on to staff the federal Irrigation Survey throughout

the west. The students measured temperature, velocity and evaporation and made soundings. When classes ended in 1889, Denver and Rio Grande Railroad station agents continued to make the necessary readings. In 1931, responsibility for the gauging station returned to the Geological Survey, which has maintained it since. The gauging station, which consists of a cable car that traverses the river to provide stream flow measurements and a small stone structure housing hydrographic instruments, was the first unit of its kind to be built anywhere; it represents a significant advance in the science of hydrology.

Ensenada *(Rio Arriba County)*

El Porvenir Community Ditch
From Los Brazos River
SR #1226 (1986), NR #86002300 (1986), ☒ 1705

Ensenada Community Ditch
From Los Brazos River to Vicinity of State Fish Hatchery
SR #1225 (1986), NR #86002303 (1986), ☒ 1705

Ramon Jaramillo House and Barn
Ensenada Rd.
SR #1222 (1986), NR #86002309 (1986), ☒ 1705

San Joaquin Church
NM 162
SR #1221 (1986), NR #86002310 (1986), ☒ 1705

Miguel Valdez Barn
San Joaquin Church Loop Rd.
SR #1220 (1986), NR #86002314 (1986), ☒ 1705

Española *(Rio Arriba County)*

Bond House
Bond St.
SR #650 (1978), NR #80002564 (1980)

Chimayó Trading Post
205 Sandia Dr.
SR #1543 (1992)

Chupaderos Canyon Small Structural Site (LA 29739)
(Los Alamos County)
SR #1762, NR #90001585 (1990), ☒ 1758

Chupaderos Mesa Village (LA 21605)
(Los Alamos County)
SR #1759, NR #90001583 (1990), ☒ 1758

Corral Canyon Pueblo Site (LA 21569, LA 29701)
SR #1761, NR #90001581 (1990), ☒ 1758

Corral Mesa Cavate Pueblo Site (LA 21566)
SR #1760, NR #90001584 (1990), ☒ 1758

Ku'ouinge Archaeological District (LA 253)
SR #1402 (1987), NR #93000674 (1993), ☒ 1703

Guaje Water/Soil Control Site
(Los Alamos County)
SR #1763, NR #90001582 (1990), ☒ 1758

La Iglesia y la Plaza de Santa Cruz de la Cañada (Holy Cross Church)
100 Block of Santa Cruz Plaza
SR #271 (1973), NR #73001148 (1973)

Galisteo *(Santa Fe County)*

Galisteo Historic District
SR #129 (1969)

Pueblo Blanco (LA 40)
SR #801 (1969)

Pueblo Colorado – North (LA 62)
SR #107 (1969)

San Lazaro (LA 91) ▲
SR #113 (1969), NR #66000490 (1966)

San Lázaro is a stone and adobe pueblo containing an estimated 1,950 rooms on both sides of the Arroyo del Chorro in the Galisteo Basin southeast of Santa Fe. The ruins on the west side of the arroyo include fourteen separate or semi-contiguous roomblocks. Ruins on the east side of the arroyo consist of four or five small units, which may be prehistoric; a historic pueblo, consisting of four buildings around a rectangular plaza; and a reservoir that may be prehistoric. The pueblo was established in the A.D. 1200s by Tewa-speaking people from northwestern New Mexico and southwestern Colorado, who, with other Galisteo Basin pueblos, are now referred to as Tano, or Southern Tewa. The west side of the pueblo was abandoned by about 1600, but people continued to live in the east side of the pueblo. The people of San Lázaro took part in the Pueblo Revolt in 1680 and, after the revolt, left the pueblo and reestablished themselves near Santa Cruz. When Diego de Vargas reconquered

New Mexico in 1692, he moved the Tano people off the arable lands, which he then redistributed to Hispanic grantees. The Tano resettled on First Mesa at Hopi in Arizona, establishing the village of Hano (from Tano). They remain there today, and still speak Tewa as well as Hopi. About 60 rooms of the San Lázaro pueblo were professionally excavated by Nels Nelson in 1912; some amateur excavation has damaged the privately-owned part of the site in recent years. The site is not accessible to the public.

Gallina *(Rio Arriba County)*

Castle of the Chama Ruin (LA 9053)
SR #94 (1969), NR #89000344 (1989), ☒ 1727

Largo/Gallina Unit House (LA 12062)
SR #348 (1974)

Nogales Cliff House Archaeological District (LA 649)
SR #252 (1972), NR #89000346 (1989), ☒ 1727

Rattlesnake Ridge Site (LA 35648)
SR #1612, NR #92001405 (1992), ☒ 1727

West Ranch Tower Site (LA 51964)
FR 313
SR #1505, NR #89000345 (1989), ☒ 1727

Glorieta *(Santa Fe County)*

SEE ALSO NORTHEAST REGION

Glorieta Pass Battlefield ▲

SR #49 (1969), NR #66000486 (1966)

In February 1862, Confederate General Henry Sibley began an invasion of New Mexico; it was the first step in the grand plan to take control of the West and extend the Confederacy to the Pacific. After defeating the Federal forces at the Battle of Valverde near Fort Craig south of Socorro, the Confederate brigade of 2,500 Texans continued up the Rio Grande Valley. They occupied Santa Fe and were moving north with the object of capturing the Colorado gold fields. The advance guard of the Confederate Army and the forces of the Union Army, consisting of Colorado troops led by Major John Chivington, met at Pigeon's Ranch near Glorieta on March 26th. After several hours of hard fighting in which Union troops pushed the Confederates back, both withdrew. They met again at Pigeon's Ranch two days later and fought all day. When seven Union companies flanked the Confederates and destroyed their supplies and wagons at the western end of the pass, the Confederates were forced to retreat down the Rio Grande and back to Texas, abandoning their campaign in the Southwest. The Confederate soldiers who died in the battle were buried on the field. Their mass grave was discovered accidentally in 1987, and the remains were removed to the National Cemetery in Santa Fe, where the Union dead are also buried. The battlefield is now a unit of Pecos National Historical Park.

Pigeon's Ranch

SR #192 (1970), GLORIETA PASS BATTLEFIELD ARCHAEOLOGICAL DISTRICT

Hernandez *(Rio Arriba County)*

Pesedeuinge Archaeological District (LA 299)

SR #1403 (1987), ⊠ 1703

Te'ewi Archaeological District (LA 252)

US 84

SR #1401 (1987), ⊠ 1703

Jemez Springs *(Sandoval County)*

Amoxiumqua Ruin (LA 481)

SR #968 (1983), NR #84002979 (1984), ⊠ 1700

Astialkwa Archaeological District (Guadalupe Mesa Ruin) (LA 1825)

SR #278 (1983), NR #84003010 (1984), ⊠ 1700

Borrego Mesa Agricultural Site (LA 56381)

SR #1733, NR #90000591 (1990), ⊠ 1728

Giusewa (Jemez State Monument)

NM 4

SR #48 (1969), NR #73001147 (1973)

Guacamayo Site (Kiabakwa) (LA 189)

SR #972 (1983), NR #84003016 (1984), ⊠ 1700

Hanakwa Ruin (LA 24972)

SR #977 (1983), NR #84003019 (1984), ☒ 1700

Holiday Mesa Logging Camp

SR #1767, NR #92001181 (1992), ☒ 1766

Hot Springs Pueblo (Hokintileta) (LA 24553)

SR #967 (1983), NR #84003022 (1984), ☒ 1700

Jemez Cave (LA 6164)

SR #1735, NR #90000593 (1990), ☒ 1728

Jemez Hot Springs Mineral Bath House

SR #761 (1979)

Jemez Pueblo

NM 4

SR #235 (1972), NR #77000926 (1977)

Kiashita Ruin (LA 46340)

SR #953 (1983), NR #84003023 (1984), ☒ 1700

Kwastiyukwa Ruin (LA 482)

SR #958 (1983), NR #84003029 (1984), ☒ 1700

Kwastiyukwa, also called Giant Footprint Ruin for a large footprint petroglyph near the site, is on a high, narrow mesa. It was a large pueblo, two or more stories high in some places, built of shaped and unshaped building stones and some adobe. There were four or five plazas, possibly 1,250 rooms, seven kivas, and what may have been a reservoir on the north end of the pueblo. Kwastiyukwa may have been occupied from the early 1300s until the Pueblo Revolt of 1680, and some roomblocks on the north end of the pueblo may indicate a reoccupation after the Revolt. This site is one of the largest and most architecturally complex of the late prehistoric and early historic period Jemez sites.

LA 24640

SR #1736, NR #90000590 (1990), ☒ 1728

LA 24790

SR #975 (1983), NR #84003001 (1984), ☒ 1700

LA 386, LA 5928

SR #970 (1983), NR #84002993 (1984), ☒ 1700

LA 44000

SR #955 (1983), NR #84002982 (1984), ☒ 1700

LA 44001

SR #981 (1983), NR #84003007 (1984), ☒ 1700

LA 483

SR #956 (1983), NR #84003050 (1984), ☒ 1700

LA 5918

SR #960 (1983), ☒ 1700

Nanishagi Ruin (LA 541)

SR #963 (1983), NR #84003033 (1984), ☒ 1700

Pueblo of Patokwa (LA 96)

SR #279 (1983), NR #84003037 (1984), ☒ 1700

Pejunkwa Ruin (LA 130)

SR #971 (1983), NR #84003039 (1984), ☒ 1700

San Juan Mesa Ruin (LA 303)

SR #117 (1969), NR #70000408 (1970), ☒ 1700

Totaskwinu Ruin (LA 479)

SR #978 (1983), NR #84003047 (1984), ☒ 1700

Tovakwa Ruin (Stable Mesa Ruin) (LA 484)

SR #976 (1983), NR #84003049 (1984), ☒ 1700

Unshagi Ruin (LA 123)
SR #964 (1983), NR #84003051 (1984), ☒ 1700

Virgin Canyon Logging Camp No. 1 (Daniels Camp) (LA 74702)
SR #1771, NR #92001180 (1992), ☒ 1766

Virgin Mesa Logging Camp No. 1 (LA 56613)
SR #1770, NR #92001182 (1992), ☒ 1766

Virgin Mesa Logging Camp No. 2 (LA 56557)
SR #1769, NR #92001183 (1992), ☒ 1766

Virgin Mesa Logging Camp No. 3 (Abousleman Mill) (LA 56507)
SR #1768, NR #92001184 (1992), ☒ 1766

Virgin Mesa Rock Art Site (LA 6164)
SR #1734, NR #90000592 (1992), ☒ 1728

Wabakwa Ruin (LA 478)
SR #965 (1983), NR #84003052 (1984), ☒ 1700

Whaashokwa (LA 24789, LA 24791)
SR #974 (1983), NR #84002997 (1984), ☒ 1700

La Bajada *(Santa Fe County)*

La Bajada Mesa Agricultural Site
SR #914 (1983), NR #83004178 (1983)

La Bajada Ruin (LA 7)
SR #384 (1975)

La Cienega *(Santa Fe County)*

Old Cienega Village Museum
NM 22
SR #387 (1975)

Cieneguilla Pueblo (LA 16)
SR #199 (1970)

El Rancho de las Golondrinas Ranch Site and Acequia System
NM 22
SR #219 (1971), NR #180002572 (1980)

La Puente *(Rio Arriba County)*

La Puente Community Ditch
From Parkview ditch to the Chama River
SR #1229 (1986), NR #86002294 (1986), ☒ 1705

La Puente Historic District
NM 112 from Terrace to Church
SR #1116 (1985), NR #85000826 (1985), ☒ 1705

Lamy *(Santa Fe County)*

Apache Canyon Railroad Bridge
Over Galisteo Creek
SR #541 (1977), NR #79001553 (1979)

Colina Verde Ruin (LA 309)
SR #97 (1969)

Pueblo of Galisteo (LA 26)
SR #111 (1969)

Pflueger General Merchandise Store and Annex Saloon
Main St.
SR #1230 (1986), NR #87000519 (1987)

Pueblo Largo (LA 183)
SR #110 (1969)

Pueblo of San Cristobal Archaeological District (LA 80)
SR #112 (1969)

Pueblo Shé (LA 239)
SR #115 (1969)

Las Trampas *(Taos County)*

Las Trampas Canoa
SR #560 (1978)

Las Trampas Historic District ▲
NM 76
SR #11 (1968), NR #67000007 (1967)

Founded as a land grant community in 1751 by Juan de Argüello and eleven other soldier-settlers from the Barrio de Analco of Santa Fe and their families, and continuously occupied for two and a half centuries, Las Trampas is one of the few Spanish colonial settlements in New Mexico which retains its plaza plan. Las Trampas was a frontier agricultural community that stood as a buffer between Apache and Ute bands east of the Sangre de Cristo mountains and the older Hispanic settlements of the Rio Grande Valley. Many of its adobe structures and its original adobe defensive wall have been lost, but the community has maintained the church, San José de Gracia, its agricultural fields and irrigation systems, the village plaza and two dozen adobe structures grouped around the plaza. In 1966 a group of preservationists formed the Las Trampas Foundation to prevent the State Highway Department from paving the highway through the walled churchyard.

San Jose de Gracia Church and Collections ▲
Las Trampas Plaza
SR #26 (1968), NR #70000415 (1970)

San José de Gracia in Las Trampas is a cruciform colonial adobe church within a walled *camposanto,* with a transept, a clerestory, a choir loft, two bell towers and two balconies (one between the bell towers and the second making a roof over the first, permitting a bell ringer to crawl out of one belfry and walk across to the other). The church was begun in 1760 when Bishop Pedro Tamarón, passing through the area, left a license for the settlers of Las Trampas to build inside their fortified plaza a church 30 *varas* (about 90 feet) long. The people of Las Trampas, including founder Juan de Argüello, then over eighty years old, went begging for alms to pay for its construction. Finally completed about 1776, the church was a *visita* of the mission of San Lorenzo de Picurís, meaning that the mis-

sion priest came to Trampas periodically to serve mass. San José de Gracia's collections, including wooden wooden altar screens that may be by noted late 18th century *santero* Pedro Antonio Fresquís, are an integral part of the church. The community of Las Trampas carried out extensive repairs on the church in the 1980s; it is now widely considered to be the best preserved Spanish Colonial church in the United States.

Lindrith *(Rio Arriba County)*

Gavilan Mercantile Company (Gavilan Trading Post)
NM 595
SR #1636 (1996)

Los Alamos *(Los Alamos County)*

Bandelier National Monument (Civilian Conservation Corps Historic District) ▲
(in Sandoval and Los Alamos Counties)
NM 4
SR #56 (1969), NR #66000042 (1966), NR #87001452 (1987)

The Bandelier Historic District comprises 31 Pueblo Revival style buildings, an entrance road, and some minor structures, including stone water fountains and faucets in the former campground, that serve Bandelier National Monument, a collection of heavily visited Anasazi ruins in Frijoles Canyon. The buildings, constructed of Bandelier formation rhyolite tuff, a local material, were designed by National Park Service architects to suggest a small southwestern village around three sides of a wooded plaza. They were built in the 1930s and 1940s by Civilian Conservation Corps (CCC) workers, who also built desks, tables, beds, wood boxes and chairs in Spanish Colonial style for the buildings. The CCC historic district, with its extraordinary unity of design and harmony with the natural setting, is a unique expression of Pueblo Revival style architecture and is also the largest collection of CCC-built structures in any national park or monument.

Guaje Site (LA 12700)
SR #856 (1982), NR #82001049 (1982)

Los Alamos Canyon Bridge
Diamond Dr. south of intersection with Trinity Dr.
SR #1665 (1997), ☒ 1661

Los Alamos County Historical Museum and Archives
1921 Juniper Ave.
SR #272 (1973), LOS ALAMOS SCIENTIFIC LABORATORY DISTRICT

Los Alamos Ranch School (The Lodge and Bathtub Row)
Bounded by Central Ave., 20th St., Nectar and 19th St.
SR #68 (1969), LOS ALAMOS SCIENTIFIC LABORATORY DISTRICT

Los Alamos Scientific Laboratory ▲
Central Ave.
SR #13 (1968), NR #66000893 (1966)

In 1942, the United States War Department selected the remote Los Alamos Ranch School for Boys (established in 1918) as the site of a scientific laboratory for the purpose of developing a nuclear fission bomb. In addition to the beneficial remoteness of the site, existing school buildings, including Fuller Lodge (designed by noted New Mexico architect John Gaw Meem), could be used for housing, shops, dining and meetings. Faculty housing near the Lodge was used by the head scientists and dubbed "Bathtub Row" for its superior facilities. The Army quickly erected temporary residences and laboratory facilities in frame buildings clustered around Ashley Pond. The first scientists arrived on "The Hill" in 1943 to work on their war-

time mission. Nuclear components were checked and assembled in the Ranch School ice house on the pond. When the Atomic Energy Commission took over Laboratory programs in 1947, it demolished temporary technical facilities and some Ranch School buildings, including the ice house. Fuller Lodge, the six private houses that constitute "Bathtub Row," a house north of the Lodge and a stone powerhouse remain. A walking tour passes most of these historic buildings.

Mesa Public Library
1742 Central Ave.
SR #1608 (1994)

Pond Cabin (Dwight Youngs' Cabin)
Pajarito Rd.
SR #1502 (1989)

Los Cerrillos *(Santa Fe County)*

Cerrillos Opera House
SR #316 (1974)

Los Cerrillos Mining District
SR #273 (1973)

Mt. Chalchihuitl Turquoise Mine
SR #566 (1978), LOS CERRILLOS MINING DISTRICT

Pueblo of San Marcos (LA 98)
NM 14
SR #114 (1969), NR #82C03326 (1982)

Waldo Coke Ovens
SR #746 (1979)

Los Ojos *(Rio Arriba County)*

George Becker House, Bunk House and Barn
La Puente Rd.
SR #1123 (1985), NR #85000777 (1985), ☒ 1705

Blanton Log House
La Puente Rd.
SR #1124 (1985), NR #85000778 (1985), ☒ 1705

T.D. Burns Store
Old NM 95
SR #764 (1980), LOS OJOS (PARKVIEW) HISTORIC DISTRICT, ^1705

Casados House
U.S. 84
SR #1117 (1985), NR #85000825 (1985), ☒ 1705

Los Ojos (Parkview) Fish Hatchery and Burns Lake Bungalow
Hatchery Rd.
SR #1113 (1984), NR #85000779 (1985), NR #85000780 (1985), ☒ 1705

Los Ojos (Parkview) Historic District
Bounded by US 84, Old US 84, Chama River Terrace and Hatchery Rd.
SR #1115 (1985), NR #85000828 (1985), ☒ 1705

Tony Manzanares House
Los Ojos Rd.
SR #1126 (1985), NR #85000829 (1985), ☒ 1705

Gilbert Martinez Barn
La Puente Rd.
SR #1122 (1985), NR #85000781 (1985), ☒ 1705

Teodoro Martinez House
La Puente Rd.
SR #1121 (1985), NR #85000782 (1985), ☒ 1705

Officer's House
La Puente Rd.
SR #1125 (1985), ☒ 1705

Our Lady of Lourdes Grotto
SR #1217 (1986), NR #86002318 (1987), ☒ 1705

First settled around 1860, the Tierra Amarilla area was a late frontier of Hispanic settlement. Most citizens were Roman Catholics or converted to Catholicism in order to join the community. There were five churches in the area, as well as numerous chapels, shrines and temporary shelters, and religious processions visited these sites every year. One such shrine is Our Lady of Lourdes Grotto, built to commemorate Josepha Burns's escape from mishap when she lost control of her buggy and her horse raced down the steep road to the town of Los Ojos. The safe conclusion of this adventure was attributed to divine intervention, and Mrs. Burns, who was married to the area's most prominent merchant, T.D. Burns, initiated the construction of a shrine, which was completed in 1919 after her death. The shrine is typical of temporary altars sponsored by wealthy families. It consists of a shallow ogee vault on a concrete foundation of rubble pumice set against a rock outcropping. It contains statues of a praying girl and Our Lady of Lourdes surrounded by votive candles and artificial flowers. Our Lady of Lourdes Grotto marks the entrance into Los Ojos and is still visited by residents and former residents of the area.

Parkview Community Ditch
From Los Brazos River to La Puente Ditch
SR #1224 (1986), NR #86002305 (1986), ☒ 1705

Sanchez/March House
West of US 84 and north of NM 95
SR #1118 (1985), NR #85000830 (1985), ☒ 1705

Fernando Trujillo, Sr. House
US 84, north of NM 95
SR #1119 (1985), NR #85000832 (1985), ☒ 1705

Manuelita Trujillo House
US 84, south of Los Brazos River
SR #1120 (1985), NR #85000831 (1985), ☒ 1705

Madrid *(Santa Fe County)*

Madrid Boarding House
NM 14
SR #454 (1976), MADRID HISTORIC DISTRICT

Madrid Historic District
NM 14
SR #356 (1974), NR #77000928 (1977)

Nambe Pueblo *(Santa Fe County)*

Nambe Archaeological District
SR #327 (1974)

Nambe Pueblo (LA 17)
SR #241 (1972), NR #74001208 (1974)

Ojo Caliente *(Taos County)*

SEE ALSO NORTHWEST REGION

Chapel of Santa Cruz de Ojo Caliente
South side of Plaza
SR #224 (1971), NR #75001174 (1975)

Howiri Archaeological District (LA 71)
SR #1405 (1987), ⊠ 1550, ⊠ 1703

Howiri-Ouinge (LA 71)
SR #911 (1983), NR #83001633 (1983), ⊠ 1703

Hupobi-ouinge (Homayo) (LA 380)
SR #910 (1983), NR #85000111 (1985), ⊠ 1703

Ojo Caliente Mineral Springs
NM 414
SR #1129 (1985), NR #85003496 (1985)

Ojo Caliente Mineral Springs is a resort complex built around five thermal springs on the edge of the village of Ojo Caliente. The complex includes the mineral springs themselves, which are of different mineral contents (iron, arsenic, sodium sulphate, lithia and soda); a stone recreation building constructed in 1860 and the earliest remaining building at the resort; an adobe Spanish Mission Revival structure built in 1917 to replace a 1912 frame hotel; and the quadrangle in front of the hotel. Other buildings at the resort, including the 1929 bath house, are utilitarian and not considered historically or architecturally significant. The mineral springs were long used by the early Hispanic settlers and probably by Pueblo people before that for their curative powers; in 1860 Antonio Joseph of Taos, recipient of the Spanish land grant where the springs are located, established a resort to take advantage of the naturally occurring waters. Ojo Caliente Mineral Springs is an early example of the development of the health, recreation and tourism industries, which began even before the railroad brought travelers to New Mexico.

Ojo Caliente Mineral Springs Barn
SR #503 (1977)

Ponsipa'akeri Archaeological District (LA 297)
SR #1406 (1987), NR #93000673 (1993), ⊠ 1703

Pose'uinge Archaeological District (LA 632)
US 285
SR #1404 (1987), ⊠ 1703

Peña Blanca *(Sandoval County)*

Kuapa Ruin (LA 3443-3444)
SR #104 (1969)

Peñasco (Taos County)

Laureano Cordova Mill
NM 75, Valdito
SR #45 (1969), NR #74001212 (1974)

Pilar *(Taos County)*

Carson School
NM 96
SR #1214 (1985), NR #86000233 (1986)

Placitas *(Sandoval County)*

Casa Acequia (LA 44534)
SR #1238 (1986), ☒ 1720

Muench House
46 Paseo de San Antonio
SR #1595 (1994)

Ojo Cuchillo (LA 50239)
SR #1242 (1986), ☒ 1720

San Jose de las Huertas (LA 25674)
SR #1249 (1986), NR #90001029 (1990), ☒ 1720

Tecolote Hill (LA 22)
SR #1251 (1986), ☒ 1720

Pojoaque *(Santa Fe County)*

Bouquet Ranch
Bouquet Ln.
SR #212 (1971), JEAN BOUQUET HISTORIC/ARCHAEOLOGICAL DISTRICT

Jean Bouquet Historic/Archaeological District
SR #888 (1982), NR #83001628 (1983)

Ignacio Roybal House
CR 84, Jacona
SR #535 (1977), NR #86000227 (1986)

Pueblo de Cochiti *(Sandoval County)*

Pueblo de Cochiti
SR #234 (1972), NR #74001205 (1974)

Kotyiti (Old Cochiti) (LA 295)
SR #281 (1973)

Pueblo of Picuris *(Taos County)*

Pueblo of Picuris (San Lorenzo Pueblo)
SR #229 (1971), NR #74001211 (1974)

Pueblo of Santa Ana *(Sandoval County)*

Canjillon Pueblo (LA 2049)
SR #1237 (1986), ☒ 1720

Pueblo of Santa Ana (Tamaya)
SR #165 (1970), NR #74001204 (1974)

Ranchos de Taos *(Taos County)*

Camino Real
SR #174 (1970)

Andrew Dasburg House and Studio
NM 3
SR #833 (1981)

Duran Chapel
SR #696 (1978)

Molino de los Duranes
SR #405 (1975)

Ranchos de Taos Plaza
Off US 64
SR #51 (1969), NR #78001830 (1978)

San Francisco de Assisi Mission Church ▲
Plaza
SR #24 (1968), NR #70000416 (1970)

Fields in the area of Ranchos de Taos, once called San Francisco de las Trampas, were cultivated in the 1700s, but Indian raids discouraged settlement until the turn of the 19th century. In 1813, Fray José Benito Pereyro, who ministered to about five hundred Taos Indians at the pueblo and perhaps three times as many Hispanics in the Taos Valley, received the license to build a chapel at the new plaza of Ranchos de Taos. The church, San Francisco de Assisi, was complete by about 1815. It is a cruciform church constructed of adobe bricks coated with adobe mud for protection, a traditional method. The church's

collections include a high altar screen with canvases from New Spain, an altar screen with an image of the Lord of Esquipulas, a crucifix and two large statues; these were inventoried in 1818 and are still in place. The altar screen is the largest remaining screen of this type in New Mexico, with around 425 square feet of surface. San Francisco de Assisi is one of the best examples of colonial adobe church architecture in New Mexico, and is a rare surviving example of early ornamentation in New Mexico churches. The massive buttresses have been painted, drawn and photographed by artists and tourists innumerable times.

St. Vrain's Mill Site
SR #790 (1980)

Vigil Torreon
NM 3
SR #409 (1975)

Red River *(Taos County)*

Orin Mallette Cabin
1501 Main St.
SR #985 (1983), NR #84003055 (1984), ☒ 1701

Sylvester M. Mallette Cabin
River St. and Copper King
SR #986 (1983), NR #84003056 (1984), ☒ 1701

Melson/Oldham Cabin
Highway 150
SR #987 (1983), NR #84003057 (1984), ☒ 1701

Pierce/Fuller House
Silver Bell Trail and High St.
SR #990 (1983), NR #84003058 (1984), ☒ 1701

Red River Miner's Hospital (Westoby House)
Jay Hawk Trail
SR #984 (1983), ☒ 1701

Red River Schoolhouse
High St.
SR #909 (1983), NR #84003059 (1984), ☒ 1701

Brigham J. Young House
Main St.
SR #988 (1983), NR #84003063 (1984), ☒ 1701

Edward P. Westoby Cabin
Jay Hawk Trail
SR #989 (1983), ☒ 1701

Rio Rancho *(Sandoval County)*

Corrales North Archaeological District (LA 319)
NM 46
SR #1383 (1987)

San Antonito *(Sandoval County)*

Sandia Cave ▲
SR #22 (1968), NR #66000487 (1966)

Sandia Cave, in the northern Sandia Mountains, is a narrow tunnel-like cave in the limestone bedrock of the east wall of Las Huertas Canyon, with an average width of about 12 feet and a length of about 381 feet. The entrance opens onto the cliff face almost 300 feet above the valley floor. Excavations in 1936-1940 yielded Folsom spear points dating to about 10,000 years ago as well as a new type of point, dubbed the Sandia point, that may be earlier than the Folsom material. An unresolved controversy surrounds the stratigraphy and dating of this site.

San Felipe Pueblo *(Sandoval County)*

San Felipe Pueblo
SR #236 (1972)

San Juan Pueblo *(Rio Arriba County)*

Rio Grande Bridge at San Juan Pueblo
NM 74 over Rio Grande
SR #1669 (1997), NR #97000738 (1997),
☒ 1661

San Gabriel de Yungue-Ouinge (LA 59) ▲
Highway 285
SR #25 (1968), NR #66000482 (1966)

From about A.D. 1450 to about 1550 the aggregated Pueblo Indian villages of the Chama Valley and the Pajarito Plateau were gradually depopulated by migration to lower elevations, arable lands and constant streams — the Rio Grande and the Chama. By about 1500, the San Juan people occupied two major towns, San Juan and *yúngé,* which means "mockingbird place" in Tewa. This site lies on a low promontory overlooking the confluence of the Rio Grande and the Chama. When explorer Coronado plundered both pueblos in 1540, he named the area Yuque-Yunque. Spanish colonizer Juan de Oñate and his advance guard reached the confluence of the Chama and the Rio Grande in 1598. They occupied the yúngé pueblo, renaming it San Gabriel and establishing the first European capital of New Mexico within the pueblo; the capital remained there until the establishment of Santa Fe in 1610. Florence Ellis, who excavated the site in the early 1960s, speculated that the people of yúngé were asked or forced to move to San Juan; that a block of rooms at yúngé was used, with little modification, to house the unmarried soldier-settlers; and that another block of rooms was modified and arranged to approximate a Spanish kitchen. The colonists also built a small chapel. When archaeologist Adolph Bandelier visited in 1892, he described the site as containing two distinct mounds separated by open space thought to be a plaza. Today, evidence of this site plan is still visible.

San Juan Pueblo
SR #254 (1972), NR #74001201 (1974)

San Ysidro *(Sandoval County)*

Big Bead Mesa (LA 15231) ▲
SR #5 (1968), NR #66000958 (1966)

Big Bead Mesa is a sandstone and marine shale formation rising sharply above the surrounding terrain. On the mesa is a planned, fortified site built by the Navajo who occupied the site from about 1745 to about 1812. The site served as a refuge from Ute attacks and Hispanic slave raids. The site consists of the remains of about ninety forked-stick and circular stone-walled *hogans* (the traditional Navajo house forms) in seven groups. A massive sandstone-slab masonry wall with a single small door, several peepholes and a small room, possibly a guard room, behind it, protects the northeastern spur of the mesa top. The site is an outstanding example of defensive planning and construction. It also shows evidence that the Navajo were adopting some Pueblo cultural patterns during this time.

Guadalupe Historic District
Guadalupe
SR #701 (1978)

Guadalupe Ruin (LA 2757)
SR #760 (1979), NR #80002571 (1980)

Santa Clara Pueblo
(Rio Arriba County)

Puye Ruins (LA 47) ▲
SR #19 (1968), NR #66000481 (1966)

Puye, a Tewa word for "where cottontail rabbits assemble," is on the Pajarito Plateau on the south rim of Santa Clara Canyon, on a mesa about a mile long. The prehistoric ruins include *cavates,* which are rooms excavated in tuff at the base of the vertical cliff where it meets the top of the talus slope; rooms built in front of these *cavates* in some areas; a large pueblo with a square interior court on the mesa top; three kivas, as well as kivas associated with the *cavate* rooms; a large reservoir excavated in the tuff; remains of garden plots and an irrigation canal. The pueblo probably dates to the late A.D. 1200s or early 1300s, a time

when large aggregated communities formed along the Rio Grande and its tributaries. By about 1600, Puye was abandoned, and its inhabitants moved down to the mouth of Santa Clara Canyon. People from nearby Santa Clara regard Puye as an ancestral pueblo.

Santa Clara Pueblo
SR #231 (1971), NR #74001199 (1974)

Tsicumo (Chicoma)
SR #132 (1969)

San Ildefonso Pueblo
(Santa Fe County)

Black Mesa (Tunyo)
SR #346 (1974)

Otowi Bridge Historic District
NM 4
SR #295 (1973), NR #75001170(1975)

Otowi Suspension Bridge
NM 4 over Rio Grande
SR #1670 (1997), NR #75001170(1997),
✉ 1661

San Ildefonso Pueblo
SR #230 (1971), NR #74001206 (1974)

Santa Fe *(Santa Fe County)*

Acequia Madre *(East Portion)*
Camino Cabra to Garcia St.
SR #205 (1970), SANTA FE HISTORIC DISTRICT

518 Agua Fria St.
SR #815 (1981), SANTA FE HISTORIC DISTRICT

532-538 Agua Fria St.
SR #805 (1981), SANTA FE HISTORIC DISTRICT

714 Agua Fria St.
SR #821 (1981), SANTA FE HISTORIC DISTRICT

733 Agua Fria St.
SR #813 (1981), SANTA FE HISTORIC DISTRICT

Jose Alarid House
338 E. DeVargas St.
SR #354 (1974), SANTA FE HISTORIC DISTRICT

Ricardo Alarid House
534 Alarid St.
SR #1022 (1984), NR #84003054 (1984), SANTA FE HISTORIC DISTRICT

Allison Dormitory
433 Paseo de Peralta
SR #1026 (1984), NR #84000431 (1984)

508 Alto St.
SR #819 (1981), SANTA FE HISTORIC DISTRICT

Archbishop Lamy's Chapel
Bishop's Lodge Rd.
SR #1395 (1987), NR #88000897 (1988)

Atchison, Topeka & Santa Fe Railway Locomotive No. 5030
St. Francis and Alta Vista
SR #367 (1975)

Atchison, Topeka & Santa Fe Railway Depot
Guadalupe at Garfield St.
SR #827 (1981), SANTA FE HISTORIC DISTRICT

Barrio de Analco Historic District ▲
Old Santa Fe Trail and E. De Vargas area
SR #4 (1968), NR #68000032 (1968)

Throughout Spanish America, a neighborhood, ward or suburb of a city is known as a *barrio.* The Barrio de Analco is one of the oldest colonial neighborhoods in the United States. First settled in the 1620s as a suburb of Santa Fe, the barrio was mostly fields and a few farmhouses. The name *analco* is a Mexican Indian word having the sense of "the lesser population on the other side of the water" suggesting that a few Tlascalan (Mexican) Indians who came to Santa Fe with Diego de Vargas may have lived here and that the neighborhood was distinguished from the area near the Santa Fe Plaza where officials and prominent citizens lived. By about 1645, the Barrio de Analco was a parish with its own chapel (San Miguel). In the eighteenth

century most of the people of the barrio were probably *genízaros,* descendants of Navajo, Apache and Plains people who had been captured by the Hispanics and who formed an important working and peasant class in the 1700s and 1800s in New Mexico. The barrio is unique as a surviving neighborhood of Spanish colonial lower class heritage.

A.M. Bergere House
135 Grant Ave.
SR #355 (1974), NR #75001166 (1975), SANTA FE HISTORIC DISTRICT

Borrego House
724 Canyon Rd.
SR #81 (1969), SANTA FE HISTORIC DISTRICT

Boyle House
321 E. De Vargas St.
SR #82 (1969), SANTA FE HISTORIC DISTRICT

Bridge of the Hidalgos
Grant Ave. and Rosario Blvd.
SR #545 (1978), SANTA FE HISTORIC DISTRICT

Camino del Monte Sol Historic District
Bounded by Acequia Madre, Camino del Monte Sol, El Caminito, and Garcia St.
SR #1112 (1984), NR #88000440 (1988)

Catanach House
722 Agua Fria St.
SR #823 (1981), SANTA FE HISTORIC DISTRICT

Chapel of San Miguel and Collections
E. De Vargas and Santa Fe Trail
SR #213 (1971), SANTA FE HISTORIC DISTRICT

Trinidad Chavez House
425 W. San Francisco St.
SR #803 (1981), SANTA FE HISTORIC DISTRICT

Conklin Estate
434-436 W. San Francisco St.
SR #806 (1981), SANTA FE HISTORIC DISTRICT

Connor Hall (NMSD)
1060 Cerrillos Rd.
SR #1470 (1988), NR #88001561 (1988), ⊠ 1707

Bruce Cooper House and Shop
Rte. 6, Box 44C
SR #1563 (1993)

Gregorio Crespin House
132 E. De Vargas St.
SR #249 (1972), NR #75001167 (1975), SANTA FE HISTORIC DISTRICT

Randall Davey House
Upper Canyon Rd.
SR #83 (1969), NR #70000409 (1970)

What is now known as the Randall Davey House was originally an adobe and stone sawmill built in 1847 by the United States Army Quartermaster to provide lumber for the construction of Santa Fe's Fort Marcy. In 1852 trapper and trader Céran St. Vrain acquired the mill at a foreclosure sale for $500. It was sold again the following year to satisfy a debt to Lucien B. Maxwell, the proprietor of the Maxwell Land Grant. By then, the two-story millhouse contained

both saw and grist mills. Artist Randall Davey bought the abandoned mill in 1920, converting it into a studio and residence. From 1920 to 1964, Davey made extensive improvements which included decorative painting by the artist on doors, interior and exterior walls and floors. The National Audubon Society bought the house in 1983, making it Audubon's southwest office. The house is set in landscaped grounds within a nature preserve accessible to the public.

Felipe Delgado House
124 W. Palace Ave.
SR #58 (1969), SANTA FE HISTORIC DISTRICT

Dendahl House
318 Guadalupe St.
SR #812 (1981), SANTA FE HISTORIC DISTRICT

Digneo/Valdez House
1231 Paseo de Peralta
SR #658 (1978), NR #78001827 (1978)

Dorman House
707 Old Santa Fe Trail
SR #752 (1979)

Dudrow House
548 Agua Fria St.
SR #822 (1981), SANTA FE HISTORIC DISTRICT

Don Gaspar Historic District
Don Gaspar Ave.
SR #891 (1982), NR #83001629 (1983)

715 Dunlap St.
SR #826 (1981), SANTA FE HISTORIC DISTRICT

El Patio Building
117 Guadalupe St.
SR #834 (1981), SANTA FE HISTORIC DISTRICT

El Zaguan
545 Canyon Rd.
SR #84 (1969), SANTA FE HISTORIC DISTRICT

Mr. and Mrs. William N. Field Residence
2 Cerro Gordo Rd.
SR #302 (1973)

First Ward School
400 Canyon Rd.
SR #707 (1978), SANTA FE HISTORIC DISTRICT

Fort Marcy Officer's Residence
116 Lincoln Ave.
SR #379 (1975), NR #75001168 (1975), SANTA FE HISTORIC DISTRICT

Fort Marcy Ruins (LA 111)
Kearney Ave.
SR #87 (1969), NR #75001169 (1975)

Hilario Gallegos House
332-334 Otero St.
SR #1002 (1984), SANTA FE HISTORIC DISTRICT

Padre Gallegos House
227-237 Washington Ave.
SR #62 (1969), SANTA FE HISTORIC DISTRICT

110 Guadalupe St.
SR #817 (1981), SANTA FE HISTORIC DISTRICT

Marcos and Nicolasa Gutierrez House
738 Agua Fria St.
SR #809 (1981), SANTA FE HISTORIC DISTRICT

Hayt/Wientge Mansion
620 Paseo de la Cuma
SR #377 (1975), NR #77000929 (1977)

Hesch House
324-326 Read St.
SR #259 (1972), SANTA FE HISTORIC DISTRICT

Francisca Hinojos House
355 E. Palace Ave.
SR #65 (1969), SANTA FE HISTORIC DISTRICT

Juan Holmes House
300 Otero St.
SR #919 (1983), SANTA FE HISTORIC DISTRICT

Hospital Building (NMSD)
1060 Cerrillos Rd.
SR #1471 (1988), NR #88001562 (1988), ⊠ 1707

Andreas Kopp House
501 Rio Grande Blvd.
SR #1003 (1984)

La Conquistadora
St. Francis Cathedral, Cathedral Pl.
SR #88 (1969), SANTA FE HISTORIC DISTRICT

La Conquistadora Chapel
St. Francis Cathedral, Cathedral Pl.
SR #141 (1970), SANTA FE HISTORIC DISTRICT

Laboratory of Anthropology
708 Camino Lejo
SR #890 (1982), NR #83001630 (1983)

Larragoite Residence
803 Agua Fria St.
SR #816 (1981), SANTA FE HISTORIC DISTRICT

Roque Lobato House
311 Washington Ave.
SR #67 (1969), SANTA FE HISTORIC DISTRICT

701 W. Manhattan Ave.
SR #808 (1981), SANTA FE HISTORIC DISTRICT (SANTA FE COUNTY)

Dorothy S. McKibben House
1099 Old Santa Fe Trail
SR #1303 (1986)

418 Montezuma Ave.
SR #807 (1981), SANTA FE HISTORIC DISTRICT

Collections at the Museum of New Mexico
116 Lincoln Ave.
SR #217 (1971)

National Park Service Southwest Regional Office ▲
Old Santa Fe Trail
SR #144 (1970), NR #70000067 (1970)

In the early 1930s, the National Park Service began a search for a centralized location to manage the growing number of Southwest national parks and monuments. The Laboratory of Anthropology donated 8.5 acres of land on condition that the National Park Service locate the headquarters in Santa Fe. The Southwest Regional Office Building followed the design principles set forth in *Park Structures and Facilities,* a 1930s National Park Service publication that called for the use of local materials, harmony with the landscape, ties to local architectural traditions and the appearance of having been constructed by native craftsman with primitive tools. Furnishings and fixtures were

designed specifically for the building and local pottery, rugs, oil paintings and etchings were purchased. The building was designed by National Park Service architect Cecil Doty and built by with labor and funding from two New Deal organizations: the Civilian Conservation Corps (CCC) and the Works Progress Administration (WPA). CCC Company 833, made up of single New Mexican men from low-income families and based in Santa Fe, did much of the work, including making 280,000 adobe bricks. The National Park Service took possession of the building in 1939, and it is still the Park Service's main office in the Southwest. The National Park Service Building has a main entrance reminiscent of Southwestern mission church facades, and its rooms enclose a central patio with a fountain and seating. It is one of the best examples of Pueblo Revival style architecture in New Mexico. It is accessible to the public, and a walking tour brochure is available at the front desk.

Old Federal Building
Cathedral Pl. at Palace St.
SR #874 (1982), NR #74001207 (1974), SANTA FE HISTORIC DISTRICT

The Oldest House
215 E. De Vargas St.
SR #468 (1976), SANTA FE HISTORIC DISTRICT

Ortiz y Ortiz Residence
573 W. San Francisco St.
SR #828 (1981), SANTA FE HISTORIC DISTRICT

Ortiz y Pino House
504 Galisteo St.
SR #1517 (1989), SANTA FE HISTORIC DISTRICT

Nicholas and Antonio Jose Ortiz Houses
306-322 W. San Francisco St.
SR #16 (1968), SANTA FE HISTORIC DISTRICT

Our Lady of Guadalupe Church
Agua Fria and Guadalupe St.
SR #72 (1969), SANTA FE HISTORIC DISTRICT

Our Lady of Light Chapel
Old Santa Fe Trail
SR #218 (1971), SANTA FE HISTORIC DISTRICT

525 E. Palace Ave.
SR #1511 (1989), SANTA FE HISTORIC DISTRICT

Palace of the Governors ▲
North side of the Plaza
SR #17 (1968), NR #66000489 (1966)

The Palace of the Governors, begun in the spring of 1610 to serve as the governor's residence and colonial capital, is the oldest European structure in Santa Fe and the oldest government building in the United States. In the 17th and 18th centuries the building was substantially larger than it is today. It contained a military chapel, a guardhouse, a residence for the governor, governmental offices, council chambers and an arsenal. Servants' quarters, barracks and stables were located to the north of the present building, and the interior patio and vegetable gardens occupied almost ten acres. After the Pueblo Revolt of 1680, when the Pueblo Indians drove the Spanish out of Santa Fe, Pueblo people lived in the Palace for twelve years, fortifying it, reducing the number of entrances and filling in exterior windows. When the Spanish, led by Diego de Vargas, took back the city in 1692, the Palace was again remodeled. A Territorial-style portal was first added around 1855. Even after a new state capital was built in 1885, the Palace continued to be the governor's residence until 1909, when the Palace was transferred to the new Museum of New Mexico. Today the Palace is a museum, open to the public, and Native American artisans sell jewelry under the portal.

Juan Jose Prada House
519 Canyon Rd.
SR #253 (1972), SANTA FE HISTORIC DISTRICT

George Cuyler Preston House
106 Faithway St.
SR #375 (1975), SANTA FE HISTORIC DISTRICT

Prince Plaza
107-117 E. Palace Ave.
SR #211 (1971), SANTA FE HISTORIC DISTRICT

Benjamin M. Read House
309 Read St.
SR #950 (1983), SANTA FE HISTORIC DISTRICT

Reredos of Our Lady of Light
Christo Rey Church, Canyon Rd. and Cristo Rey St.
SR #89 (1979), NR #70000411 (1970), SANTA FE HISTORIC DISTRICT

Rio Grande Depot
Guadalupe St. at Garfield St.
SR #350 (1974), SANTA FE HISTORIC DISTRICT

Juan Rodriguez House
Cerro Gordo and Gonzales
SR #76 (1969)

Rosario Chapel and Cemetery
Guadalupe St.
SR #90 (1969), SANTA FE HISTORIC DISTRICT

Jose Rafael Roybal House
541 Agua Fria St.
SR #814 (1981), SANTA FE HISTORIC DISTRICT

Olive Rush Studio
630 Canyon Rd.
SR #303 (1973), SANTA FE HISTORIC DISTRICT

406 W. San Francisco St.
SR #804 (1981), SANTA FE HISTORIC DISTRICT

447 W. San Francisco St.
SR #818 (1981), SANTA FE HISTORIC DISTRICT

450 W. San Francisco St.
SR #811 (1981), SANTA FE HISTORIC DISTRICT

637 1/2 W. San Francisco St.
SR #810 (1981), SANTA FE HISTORIC DISTRICT

Sandoval House
671-673 W. San Francisco St.
SR #825 (1981), SANTA FE HISTORIC DISTRICT

Santa Fe Builders Supply Company (SANBUSCO) Building
500 Montezuma Ave.
SR #820 (1981), SANTA FE HISTORIC DISTRICT

Santa Fe County Courthouse
102 Grant Ave.
SR #1279 (1986), SANTA FE HISTORIC DISTRICT, ☒ 1722

Santa Fe Historic District
Bounded by Camino Cabra, Camino de las Animas, W. Manhattan Ave., S. St. Francis Dr. and Griffin St.
SR #260 (1972), NR #73001150 (1973)

Santa Fe Plaza ▲
SR #27 (1968), NR #66000491 (1966), SANTA FE HISTORIC DISTRICT

When Juan de Oñate occupied the Indian Pueblo of yúngé and named it San Gabriel in 1598, he ignored the 1573 Laws of the Indies, which prohibited encroaching on Indian lands. Pedro de Peralta, who succeeded Oñate as Governor of New Mexico, moved the capital south thirty miles in 1610 to a level site near a tributary of the Rio Grande. The place was called *ogaponge* or "over at the shells by the water" in Tewa, and was probably a small Spanish herding camp. The Laws of the Indies required a grid of streets and a central plaza with a church and government buildings. Originally an unbroken open rectangular space extending all the way to the parish church (now the St. Francis Cathedral) on the east, the Plaza was used for military and religious functions, daily markets and social gatherings. In 1821 when Santa Fe Trail was established, the Plaza served as its terminus. Caravans of merchandise from the east were unloaded at a customs house on the east side. When the Confederate forces occupied Santa Fe for two weeks during the Civil War, their flag flew over the Plaza until their retreat after the Battle of Glorieta Pass. The cornerstone of the central monument in the Plaza commemorates the Civil War battle, as well as Indian conflicts, and was laid in 1867. The Plaza has seen numerous alterations; its present configuration is based on a plan drawn in 1973 by New Mexico architect John Gaw Meem, who emphasized simplicity and open space thought generally consistent with the original appearance. The Plaza has been the center of Santa Fe for nearly four hundred years.

Santa Fe River Sites (LA 16769)
SR #200 (1970)

Santa Fe Waterworks Reservoir (Two Mile Dam and Reservoir)
Upper Canyon Rd.
SR #577 (1978)

School Building No. 2 (NMSD)
1060 Cerrillos Rd.
SR #1469 (1988), NR #88001560 (1988), ☒ 1707

Scottish Rite Temple
463 Paseo de Peralta
SR #924 (1983), NR #87000424 (1987)

Second Ward School
312 Sandoval St.
SR #516 (1977), NR #78001828 (1978), SANTA FE HISTORIC DISTRICT

Sena Plaza
E. Palace Ave.
SR #91 (1969), SANTA FE HISTORIC DISTRICT

Jose D. Sena House
202 Closson St.
SR #824 (1981), SANTA FE HISTORIC DISTRICT

Seton Castle (part of Seton Village ▲)
US 84
SR #119 (1969)

Seton Village ▲
US 84
SR #282 (REMOVED), NR #66000492 (1966)

Artist, author and scientist Ernest Thompson Seton is best remembered as one of the great American naturalists and as the chairman of the committee that introduced the Boy Scout movement into the United States. Born in England in 1860, he lived and traveled in Canada and the United States, establishing Seton Village six miles southeast of Santa Fe in 1930. The 43-acre Seton Village site on the western slope of a row of hills was the core area of Seton's original property of 2,500 acres. It comprises a group of structures including several houses, a print shop, craft shop and barn around an oval plaza and along its approach lane. The lane crosses a main road and proceeds 75 yards uphill to the main house. Known as "The Castle," this twenty-room structure was designed in 1934 as a combination home, museum, library, art gallery and institute for creative people in every discipline. Seton lived and taught at Seton Village until his death in 1946. There are two recent adobe houses below the castle and the site also includes a Navajo-style hogan and a Pueblo-inspired kiva north of the castle. Seton Village is significant for its association with Seton, who helped shaped present-day conservation philosophy.

Eugenie Shonnard House
1411 Paseo de Peralta
SR #320 (1974), NR #75001171 (1975), DON GASPAR HISTORIC DISTRICT

Sol y Sombra
4108 Old Santa Fe Trail
SR #615 (1978)

Spanish and Mexican Period Documentary Collections
404 Montezuma St.
SR #289 (1973)

Spanish Log Cabin
Upper Canyon Rd.
SR #256 (1972)

Spiegelberg/Spitz House
327 E. Palace Ave.
SR #223 (1971), NR #73001151 (1973), SANTA FE HISTORIC DISTRICT

Stone Warehouse
316 Guadalupe St.
SR #261 (1972), SANTA FE HISTORIC DISTRICT

Superintendent's Residence (NMSD)
1060 Cerrillos Rd.
SR #1472 (1988), NR #88001563 (1988), ☒ 1707

Supreme Body Shop
326 Guadalupe St.
SR #831 (1981), SANTA FE HISTORIC DISTRICT

Roque Tudesqui House
129-135 E. De Vargas St.
SR #258 (1972), SANTA FE HISTORIC DISTRICT

Pinckney R. Tully House
136 Grant Ave.
SR #79 (1969), NR #74001209 (1974), SANTA FE HISTORIC DISTRICT

United States Courthouse
Federal Pl.
SR #244 (1972), NR #73001152 (1973), SANTA FE HISTORIC DISTRICT

Peter Van Dresser House
1002 ½ Canyon Rd.
SR #835 (1981), SANTA FE HISTORIC DISTRICT

Carlos Vierra House
1002 Old Pecos Trail
SR #712 (1979), NR #79001554 (1979)

Donaciano Vigil House
518 Alto St.
SR #80 (1969), NR #72000811 (1972)

Wheelwright Museum of the American Indian
704 Camino Lejo
SR #1533 (1990), NR #90001917 (1990), ☒ 1521

Professor J.A. Wood House
511 Armijo St.
SR #851 (1982), SANTA FE HISTORIC DISTRICT

Santo Domingo Pueblo *(Sandoval County)*

Santo Domingo Pueblo
SR #237 (1972), NR #73001145 (1973)

Stanley *(Santa Fe County)*

West Otto Site (LA 49928)
SR #245 (1972)

Talpa *(Taos County)*

Talpa Altar Screen
Chapel at Talpa, NM 3
SR #78 (1969)

Taos *(Taos County)*

Governor Bent House
Bent St.
SR #50 (1969), NR #78001831 (1978)

Ernest L. Blumenschein House ▲
Ledoux St.
SR #6 (1968), NR #66000495 (1966)

Ernest Blumenschein and Bert Phillips were the first Anglo-American Taos artists, arriving in 1898, and co-founders of the Taos Society of Artists in 1914, an institution which led to Taos' importance as an art colony. Blumenschein bought what is now known as the Blumenschein house from another Taos artist, Herbert Dutton, in 1919. The eleven-room adobe may have been built prior to 1821. It is now a museum which reflects the life and career of a significant artist and his circle of friends, giving us a view of the Taos colony of artists in the early years of New Mexico's statehood.

Kit Carson House ▲
Kit Carson Ave.
SR #8 (1968), NR #66000948 (1966)

During the 19th century, a number of the fur trappers or "mountain men," the first Anglo-Americans to explore the American west, settled in northern New Mexico. Of these mountain men, Kit Carson was perhaps the most famous. Born in Kentucky

in 1809, Carson was a trapper, guide, Indian agent, and Army officer, instrumental in subduing the Apache, Navajo and Kiowa Indians. When he married Josefa Jaramillo, daughter of a prominent Taos family, in 1843, Carson bought a single-story U-shaped adobe house, built around a courtyard, which had been constructed in 1825. At least six of their eight children were born there. After Carson died in Colorado in 1868, his body was brought back to Taos, and visitors often stop at his grave in Kit Carson Park. The Carson House was both his home and a fine example of Spanish Colonial and Territorial architectural features.

Chapel of San Miguel del Valle
Off NM 76
SR #246 (1972)

Nicholai Fechin House
NM 3
SR #718 (1979), NR #79001558 (1979)

Leon Gaspard House and Collections
Raton Rd.
SR #705 (1978), NR #79001559 (1979)

Harwood Foundation of the University of New Mexico
Ledoux St.
SR #362 (1975), NR #76001200 (1976)

E. Martin Hennings House and Studio Historic District
Dolan St. and Kit Carson Rd.
SR #1530 (1990), NR #90001028 (1990)

La Loma Plaza Historic District
NM 240
SR #861 (1982), NR #82003339 (1982)

Mabel Dodge Luhan House ▲
Luhan Lane
SR #540 (1977), NR #78001832 (1978)

Mabel Ganson Evans Dodge Sterne Luhan, friend of prominent artists, memorialist and author, was born in New York in 1879. She was well-known in the New York art scene, holding salons for artists and writers, before moving to Santa Fe in 1917 to join her third husband, painter Maurice Sterne. After the move to Taos, they divorced and Mabel bought land adjoining the Taos Reservation in 1918. There were two small adobe houses, dating to the late 1700s or early 1800s, on the land, which Mabel began remodeling and enlarging into what she called the Big House and the St. Teresa House. The houses were built around a central court with traditional methods and blended Pueblo, Spanish Colonial and Tuscan styles; they were completed in 1922.

During construction, Mabel had developed a relationship with Tony Lujan, the Taos Pueblo man who was the foreman of the construction crew. When Mabel and Tony were married the year following completion, Mabel took the anglicized name Luhan. Mabel later built five smaller houses on the property and her home became a mecca for artists and writers, including D.H. Lawrence and Willa Cather; the latter wrote *Death Comes for the Archbishop* while staying at the Big House. Mabel was the author of several books including *Lorenzo in Taos,* written in 1932 about her friendship with D.H. Lawrence. Her house reflects an important stage in the emergence of Taos and New Mexico as a haven for artists. The house is now a bed and breakfast.

Manby House
Camino del Pueblo del Norte
SR #763 (1980), TAOS DOWNTOWN HISTORIC DISTRICT

Severino Martinez House
Lower Ranchitos Rd.
SR #202 (1970), NR #73001153 (1973)

Morada de Nuestra Senora de Guadalupe
US 64
SR #368 (1975), NR #76001201 (1976)

Rio Grande Gorge Bridge
NM 111 over Rio Grande Gorge
SR #1664 (1997), NR #97000733 (1997), ⊠ 1661

Collection at the Millicent Rogers Foundation
SR #216 (1971)

San Ysidro Oratorio
NM 240, Los Cordovas
SR #783 (1980), NR #84003060 (1984)

Taos County Courthouse
Northeast side of Taos Plaza
SR #1272 (1986), TAOS DOWNTOWN HISTORIC DISTRICT, ⊠ 1722

Taos Downtown Historic District
NM 3 and NM 240
SR #860 (1982), NR #82003340 (1982)

Taos Inn
Pueblo del Norte
SR #802 (1981), NR #82003341 (1982)

Taos Pueblo ◎ ▲
SR #243 (1972), NR #66000496 (1966)

The earliest known settlements in the Taos Valley were pithouse villages that date to about A.D. 1000-1200. The Indians then moved into numerous, small "unit pueblos," some with kivas. Population aggregation continued with major centers of

population during the years 1250 to 1350 at Pot Creek and near modern Picuris Pueblo. Around 1350, a community usually called "Cornfield Taos" was established about a quarter of a mile northeast of the present site; it was abandoned around 1500. The present Pueblo of Taos dates to before 1540; it sits on a plateau at the base of the Sangre de Cristo mountain range and consists of two large multistoried adobe house clusters (North and South Houses) on either side of the Rio Pueblo de Taos. Taos Pueblo was historically a place of trade between the Rio Grande pueblos and the plains tribes. When the Spanish arrived, Taos Pueblo was hosting an annual fall trade fair. The Indian Reorganization Act of 1934 changed the use of the pueblo by discouraging communalism and encouraging an orientation outside the pueblo. Increasingly, the Taos people built houses outside the pueblo wall and the pueblo evolved from being the community itself to being the sacred focal point of the expanding community. The Taos people have been central to several attempts to drive foreigners out of New Mexico. Popé, a medicine man from San Juan Pueblo, went to live in Taos and planned the 1680 Revolt in the Taos kivas. Taos was in the forefront of the uprising of 1847 (the old church was cannonaded by American troops and left in ruins during the decisive battle here). Taos Pueblo has been designated a World Heritage Site for its global significance.

Tesuque *(Santa Fe County)*

Pueblo of Tesuque
SR #222 (1971), NR #73001149 (1973)

Tierra Amarilla *(Rio Arriba County)*

El Vado Dam
On Chama River and NM 112
SR #550 (1978)

Rio Arriba County Courthouse
NM 162
SR #1267 (1986), TIERRA AMARILLA HISTORIC DISTRICT, ⊠ 1722

Tierra Amarilla Community Ditch
Through central village
SR #1223 (1986), NR #86002307 (1986), ⊠ 1705

Tierra Amarilla Historic District
Central village and along La Puente Rd.
SR #1216 (1986), NR #86002327 (1986), ⊠ 1705

Tres Piedras *(Taos County)*

Old Tres Piedras Administrative Site
West of US 285
SR #1709, NR #92000341 (1993)

Tres Piedras Railroad Water Tower
Off US 285
SR #579 (1978), NR #79001560 (1979)

Truchas *(Rio Arriba County)*

Nuestra Señora del Rosario Church
SR #406 (1975)

Vallecitos *(Sandoval County)*

Boletsakwa Ruin (LA 136)
SR #954 (1983), NR #84003011 (1984), ☒ 1700

Boletukwa and Little Boletukwa (LA 135)
SR #962 (1983), NR #84002989 (1984), ☒ 1700

Cactus Hill (LA 403)
SR #982 (1983), NR #84003008 (1984), ☒ 1700

Exchange Hotel Complex
Bland
SR #949 (1983)

Kiatsi-kwa (LA 137)
SR #979 (1983), NR #84003002 (1984), ☒ 1700

Kiatsukwa Ruin (LA 132, LA133)
SR #961 (1983), SR #966 (1983), NR #84003026 (1984), ☒ 1700

LA 385, LA 5930
SR #969 (1983), NR #84002991 (1984), ☒ 1700

LA 46341
SR #957 (1983), NR #84002984 (1984), ☒ 1700

LA 5920
SR #959 (1983), NR #84002986 (1984), ☒ 1700

San Juan Ruin (LA 128)
SR #980 (1983), NR #84003005 (1984), ☒ 1700

Wahajhamka Ruin (LA 24788)
SR #973 (1983), NR #84003053 (1984), ☒ 1700

White Rock *(Los Alamos County)*

Navawi (LA 214, LA 257, LA 1105)
SR #857 (1982), NR #82001052 (1982)

Pajarito Springs Site (LA 12701)
SR #858 (1982), NR #82001050 (1982)

White Rock Canyon Archaeological District (LA 71256)
NM 4
SR #1519 (1990), NR #90000717 (1990), NR #92000501 (1992)

Youngsville *(Rio Arriba County)*

Tsiping Archaeological District (LA 301)
SR #124 (1969), NR #70000405 (1970), ☒ 1703

Zia Pueblo *(Sandoval County)*

Ko-ah'-sai-ya Ruin (LA 384)
SR #347 (1974)

Zia Pueblo
SR #232 (1971), NR #73001146 (1973)

Northeast

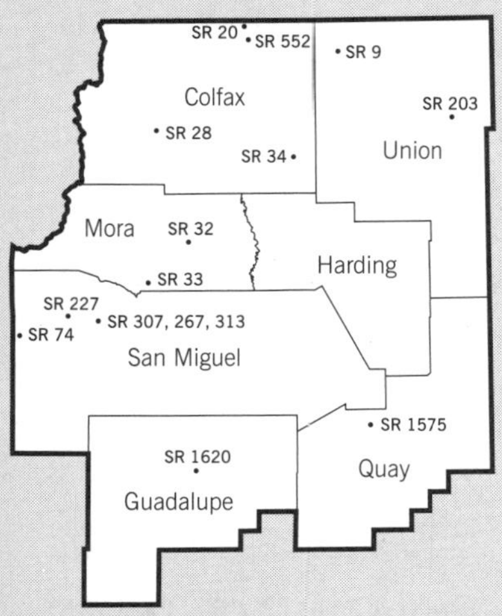

Northeastern New Mexico is a dramatic landscape stretching from the state's highest mountains to the endless rolling prairies that form the western edge of the Great Plains. Crossed by those near mythic rivers of cowboy Americana, the Pecos and the Canadian, the northeast region comprises huge, empty stretches of grassland beneath immense skies. The history of the region has been dominated by three of the most important transportation corridors in New Mexico: the Santa Fe Trail; the Atchison, Topeka, and Santa Fe Railroad; and Route 66. The registered sites of this region include the camps, trail ruts and landmarks of the Santa Fe Trail; the commercial districts and neighborhoods of the railroad era Victorian town of Las Vegas; the Old West flavored sites of Cimarron; and the vast cattle empires of the Maxwell Grant and later ranches. In addition to these, places as varied as Ft. Union, the mining town of Raton, the first documented Paleoindian site at Folsom, and the WPA-built dam at Conchas, form the fascinating historical landscape of northeastern New Mexico.

Abbott *(Colfax County)*

Stephen W. Dorsey Mansion

Off U.S. 56

SR #34 (1968), NR #70000399 (1970)

Stephen Dorsey was a Civil War veteran, corporate president and former U.S. Senator from Arkansas who emigrated to New Mexico and began building his home at Chico Springs in the late 1870s. The mansion consists of two distinct but connected elements: one a beautifully detailed log home with squared and chinked log walls and a wooden shingled roof built in 1878 to 1879, and the other a formal home with hewn sandstone walls, a tower and a composition roof built in 1884. The two sections contain thirty-six rooms, seven fireplaces (one onyx and one marble), six stairways, a dining room, an art gallery, a library and a billiard room, servants' quarters upstairs, and a wine cellar. The sandstone tower features sculpted portraits of Dorsey, his wife and brother, and two gargoyles representing Dorsey's political enemy James Blaine. The mansion originally had lavishly landscaped grounds and fountains. While building his home, Dorsey

was tried for his role in the Star Route mail fraud, one of the national scandals of the Grant administration. Defended by Robert Ingersoll, he was acquitted in 1883. Following various financial reverses, Dorsey lost the mansion and his ranch to foreclosure in 1893 and left New Mexico. The mansion is architecturally significant in its combination of Gothic Revival and Victorian Italian villa elements. Dorsey's house, and his life, mirrored America's Gilded Age.

Amistad *(Union County)*

Amistad Gymnasium (Amistad School)
NM 402
SR #1622 (1996), NR #96000264 (1996), ✉ 1617

Anton Chico *(Guadalupe County)*

Anton Chico Abajo Historic District
NM 119
SR #1176 (1985), NR #86002334 (1986), ✉ 1176

Hormigoso Irrigation Ditch and Dam
SR #555 (1978)

Tecolotito Dam
SR #578 (1978)

Bueyeros *(Harding County)*

Bueyeros School
NM 102, west of Bueyeros Church
SR #1621 (1996), NR #96000265 (1996), ✉ 1617

Sacred Heart Church
NM 102
SR #138 (1969)

Cimarron *(Colfax County)*

Cimarron Historic District
Along NM 21
SR #187 (1970), NR #73001140 (1973)

North Ponil Canyon Archaeological District
SR #907 (1982)

Villa Philmonte Historic District
Philmont Scout Ranch
SR #1611 (1995), NR #95001018 (1995)

Aztec Mill
Old Town
SR #3 (1968), CIMARRON HISTORIC DISTRICT

Dawson Cemetery (Evergreen Cemetery)
US 64 and the Dawson Rd.
SR #1542 (1992), NR #92000249 (1992)

Dawson Coke Ovens
SR #699 (1978)

Former Colfax County Courthouse in Cimarron
16th St. and Collinson
SR #1262 (1986), CIMARRON HISTORIC DISTRICT, ✉ 1722

Philturn Rocky Mountain Scout Camp
SR #908 (1982)

The Ring Place (LA 65365)
FR 1918A
SR #1495 (1989), NR #88001054 (1988)

St. James Hotel
Main Street
SR #28 (1968), CIMARRON HISTORIC DISTRICT

The two-story stuccoed adobe St. James Hotel was built in the 1870s by Henry Lambert, a former White House chef who had served Presidents Abraham Lincoln and Ulysses Grant. Cimarron was an important

stop on the Cimarron Branch of the Santa Fe Trail and was an outfitting point for prospectors, trappers and hunters. Buffalo Bill Cody organized his "Wild West Show" in Cimarron and subsequently toured the United States and Europe. He spent Christmas in the hotel whenever possible and gave Christmas parties here for the children of Cimarron. Ranchers, traders and outlaws, including Clay Allison, also patronized the St. James, which is still a hotel.

Clayton *(Union County)*

Clayton Public Schools Historic District (Campus No. 1)
6th St. and Cedar St.
SR #1623 (1996), NR #96000269 (1996),
☒ 1617

Eklund Hotel
15 Main St.
SR #220 (1971)

Herzstein Memorial Museum (Methodist Church)
2nd St. and Walnut St.
SR #1508 (1989)

Rabbit Ears (Clayton Complex) Archaeological District (LA 38648, LA 48827) ▲
SR #203 (1970), NR #66000499 (1966)

After 1821, the Santa Fe Trail's Cimarron Cutoff was widely used as an alternate route to avoid the treacherous Mountain Branch through Raton Pass. It was preferred for its gentler grades despite a 58-mile portion from the Arkansas River to Cimarron without water. There are two major landmarks along this part of the Santa Fe Trail: Rabbit Ears Mountain and Round Mound (Mt. Clayton), as well as three camp sites (McNees Crossing, Turkey Creek Camp and Rabbit Ears Creek Camp). The registered historic site called the Clayton Complex includes all of these. Rabbit Ears is a conspicuous double-peaked mountain, visible for four days journey, which guided wagon trains from the Upper Spring of the Cimarron in Oklahoma to the camp sites, with their

constant water and rich meadows. Wagon trains often stayed over for a day at the Rabbit Ears Creek Camp to refresh their animals. The Cimarron Cutoff was no longer used after 1878 when the railroad advanced from Kansas. This area then developed as ranching and farming land around the town of Clayton. The landmarks, camps and trail route have remained relatively open and untouched within local ranches.

Union County Courthouse
Court St.
SR #408 (1975), NR #87000891 (1987),
☒ 1722

Cleveland *(Mora County)*

Cassidy Mill
NM 3
SR #400 (1975), NR #78001818 (1978)

Daniel Cassidy and Sons General Merchandise Store
NM 3
SR #518 (1977), NR #79001541 (1979)

Desiderio Valdez House
Rio de la Casa Rd.
SR #1526 (1990), NR #90001059 (1990), ⊠ 1521

Conchas *(San Miguel County)*

Bell Ranch Headquarters
Vicinity of Conchas
SR #133 (1969), NR #70000407 (1970)

Conchas Dam
Vicinity of Conchas
SR #547 (1978)

Indian Writings
Vicinity of Conchas Lake
SR #497 (1977)

Cuervo *(Guadalupe County)*

Route 66: Cuervo to NM 156
SR #1576 (1993), NR #93001206 (1993), ⊠ 1564

Route 66, State Maintained: Montoya to Cuervo (Ozark Trail) *(in Quay County)*
SR #1676 (1997), NR #97001395 (1997), ⊠ 1564

Eagle Nest *(Colfax County)*

Eagle Nest Dam
SR #549 (1978), NR #79001537 (1979)

Folsom *(Union County)*

Folsom Hotel
Grand Ave. and Wall St.
SR #85 (1969), NR #87000726 (1987)

Folsom Man Site (LA 8121) ▲
(in Colfax County)
SR #9 (1968), NR #66000473 (1966)

Around 8000 B.C., what is now known as the Folsom Man Site was a marsh in which Pleistocene bison were mired and killed by early hunters. The site was discovered in 1908 by Crowfoot Ranch foreman George McJunkin, a self-educated black cowboy and former slave. Four years after his death in 1922, friends to whom he had shown the area showed bones from the site to J.D. Figgins, the director of the Colorado (now Denver) Museum of Natural History. This led to a 1927 excavation which found a spear point, firmly embedded between two bison ribs, that dated the human presence in the Americas to at least ten thousand years ago. This association of human-made tools with the bones of an animal that became extinct at the end of the Ice Age provided the first definite proof of the presence of man in North America during the Late Pleistocene era. The site is not accessible to the public.

Folsom Museum
Main St.
SR #86 (1979)

Glorieta *(San Miguel County)*

SEE ALSO NORTH-CENTRAL REGION

Glorieta Baldy Lookout Tower
Santa Fe National Forest
SR #1451 (1988), NR #87C02492 (1988),
☒ 1708

Las Vegas *(San Miguel County)*

Acequia Madre
Vicinity of Taos St.
SR #1094 (1984), NR #87001118 (1987),
☒ 1715

Arturo Angel House
926 S. Pacific
SR #1043 (1984), NR #85002604 (1985),
☒ 1715

Arthur Lewis and E.N. Charles House
807 Douglas Ave.
SR #1041 (1984), NR #85002605 (1985),
☒ 1715

Atchison, Topeka & Santa Fe Railway Locomotive No. 1129
Park at Mills and Grand Ave.
SR #343 (1974)

Atchison, Topeka & Santa Fe Railway Roundhouse
Railroad Ave.
SR #345 (1974), NR #85002621 (1985),
☒ 1715

Baca/Korte House
615 S. Pacific
SR #1091 (1984), NR #85002658 (1985),
☒ 1715

Bank of Las Vegas
622 Douglas Ave.
SR #443 (1976), DOUGLAS/SIXTH ST. HISTORIC DISTRICT

Bean/Newlee House
1045 5th St.
SR #1028 (1984), NR #85002625 (1985),
☒ 1715

Henry Blattman House
1710 8th St.
SR #1072 (1984), ☒ 1715

Bridge Street Historic District
100 block of Bridge St.
SR #339 (1974), NR #78001824 (1978),
☒ 1715

1214 Bridge
SR #1027 (1984), NR #85002660 (1985),
☒ 1715

Brown and Manzanares Company Building
600 Railroad Ave.
SR #321 (1974), RAILROAD AVENUE HISTORIC DISTRICT, ☒ 1715

The Site of Camp Luna (LA 54486)
SR #340 (1974)

Castañeda Hotel
524 Railroad Ave.
SR #307 (1974), RAILROAD AVENUE HISTORIC DISTRICT, ☒ 1715

The Castañeda was built in 1898-99 as one of the luxury hotels of the Fred Harvey system, which was established to serve railway passengers. Fred Harvey's hotels, lunchrooms and dining rooms, providing excellent food and clean accommodations, were immensely popular in regions of the West that had never seen such refinements, and many of his strictly chaperoned "Harvey Girl" waitresses eventually married cowboys, ranchers and engineers. There were sixteen Harvey Houses in New

Mexico. Only four, the Castañeda, the Clovis Hotel, the Montezuma Hotel, and the Belen Harvey House, are still standing. The Castañeda Hotel was built in 1899 and replaced Las Vegas's first Harvey House lunchroom. Since more than a third of Theodore Roosevelt's Rough Rider Regiment were recruited in New Mexico, with many from the Las Vegas area, to serve in the Spanish-American War, Roosevelt hosted the first annual reunion of the Rough Riders at the Castañeda in 1899. The Castañeda operated as a Harvey Hotel until 1948. Though the second story is used as apartments, the public can still visit the bar on the ground floor.

921 Chavez
SR #1090 (1984), NR #85002653 (1985), ☒ 1715

Lowery Clevenger House
1013 2nd St.
SR #1032 (1984), NR #85002594 (1985), ☒ 1715

1116 Columbia
SR #1079 (1984), NR #85002641 (1985), ☒ 1715

James Cook House
1017 11th St.
SR #1080 (1984), NR #85002647 (1985), ☒ 1715

Crockett Building
600-604 Douglas Ave.
SR #448 (1976), DOUGLAS/SIXTH STREET HISTORIC DISTRICT

Dice Apartments
210-218 N. Plaza
SR #265 (1972), LAS VEGAS PLAZA HISTORIC DISTRICT, ☒ 1715

Distrito de las Escuelas
S. Pacific St. and S. Gonzales St.
SR #293 (1973), NR #80002567 (1980), ☒ 1715

Douglas Avenue School
900 Douglas St.
SR #894 (1982), NR #83001625 (1983)

810 Douglas
SR #1040 (1984), NR #85002603 (1985), ☒ 1715

812 Douglas
SR #1039 (1984), NR #85002602 (1985), ☒ 1715

814 Douglas
SR #1038 (1984), NR #85002601 (1985), ☒ 1715

818 Douglas
SR #1037 (1984), NR #85002600 (1985), ☒ 1715

822 Douglas
SR #1036 (1984), NR #85002599 (1985), ⊠ 1715

Douglas/Sixth Street Historic District
Bounded by Grand, Lincoln, 7th St. and University Ave.
SR #893 (1982), NR #83001626 (1983), ⊠ 1715

1513 Eighth
SR #1068 (1984), NR #85002634 (1985), ⊠ 1715

1616 Eighth
SR #1073 (1984), NR #85002645 (1985), ⊠ 1715

1717 Eighth
SR #1071 (1984), NR #85002646 (1985), ⊠ 1715

El Fidel Hotel
Douglas and Grande Ave.
SR #449 (1976), DOUGLAS/SIXTH STREET HISTORIC DISTRICT

Eldorado Hotel (Vicente Salazar Senior Citizen's Center)
514 Grand Ave.
SR #1058 (1984), NR #85002626 (1985), ⊠ 1715

1007 Eleventh St.
SR #1081 (1984), NR #85002648 (1985), ⊠ 1715

Exchange Hotel – Remains
1717 W. Plaza
SR #266 (1972), LAS VEGAS PLAZA HISTORIC DISTRICT, ⊠ 1715

Fidelity Building
801 7th St.
SR #450 (1976), NORTH NEW TOWN HISTORIC DISTRICT

Romaine Fielding and Tom Mix Studio
920 Gallinos St.
SR #330 (1974), LINCOLN PARK HISTORIC DISTRICT, ⊠ 1715

First Baptist Church
700 University Ave.
SR #1052 (1984), NR #85002612 (1985), ⊠ 1715

First National Bank Building
181 Bridge St.
SR #310 (1974), LAS VEGAS PLAZA HISTORIC DISTRICT, ⊠ 1715

First United Presbyterian Church in Las Vegas
1000 Douglas Ave.
SR #432 (1976)

Eugenio Gatignole House
1114 S. Gonzales
SR #1042 (1984), NR #85002606 (1985), ⊠ 1715

Gazette Complex
235 Moreno St.
SR #694 (1978), DISTRITO DE LAS ESCUELAS, ⊠ 1715

12 Grand Avenue
SR #1055 (1984), NR #85002622 (1985), ⊠ 1715

16 Grand Avenue
SR #1056 (1984), NR #85002623 (1985), ⊠ 1715

Gross, Blackwell & Company Building
420 Railroad Ave.
SR #323 (1974), RAILROAD AVENUE HISTORIC DISTRICT, ⊠ 1715

Hebrew Temple (Newman Chapel)
903 8th St.
SR #317 (1974), NORTH NEW TOWN HISTORIC DISTRICT

Esperansa Herrera House
2231 Church St.
SR #1047 (1984), NR #85002613 (1985), ☒ 1715

Ilfeld Auditorium (NMHU)
University Ave.
SR #342 (1974), NR #80002568 (1980), ☒ 1715

Ilfeld Law Office Building
220 N. Plaza
SR #538 (1977), LAS VEGAS PLAZA HISTORIC DISTRICT, ☒ 1715

Charles Ilfeld Building
Las Vegas Plaza
SR #140 (1970), LAS VEGAS PLAZA HISTORIC DISTRICT, ☒ 1715

Charles Ilfeld Memorial Chapel
Masonic Cemetery, Colonias and Romero
SR #1083 (1984), NR #85002657 (1985), ☒ 1715

Jesuit School Building
1409 S. Pacific Ave.
SR #294 (1973), DISTRITO DE LAS ESCUELAS, ☒ 1715

Johnsen House
1523 8th St.
SR #1069 (1984), NR #85002635 (1985), ☒ 1715

Johnsen Memorial Mortuary
801 Douglas Ave.
SR #451 (1976), NR #85002607 (1985), ☒ 1715

Jack Johnson's Training Camp
2008 N. Gonzales
SR #452 (1976), OLD TOWN RESIDENTIAL HISTORIC DISTRICT

Senator Andrieus A. Jones House
1021 5th St.
SR #457 (1976), NORTH NEW TOWN HISTORIC DISTRICT

Las Vegas Armory
917 Douglas Ave.
SR #334 (1974)

Las Vegas Plaza Historic District
Las Vegas Plaza and vicinity
SR #267 (1972), NR #74001202 (1974), ☒ 1715

In 1835 twenty-five families from San Miguel del Vado to the west of what is now Las Vegas petitioned for a land grant on the Gallinas River in the *Vegas Grandes.* They had been using the *Vegas Grandes,* or great meadows, as a grazing area as early as the 1820s. Las Vegas Plaza, the center of the community, was officially laid out on April 6, 1835. It had a defensive wall (which probably did not last long), a well, and a ditch that brought water from the hills to the west. In 1846 when Brigadier General Stephen Watts Kearney rode into the plaza and proclaimed New Mexico a territory of the United States, Las Vegas was described as "an assemblage of mud houses covering a square of fifteen acres." The railroad first reached Las Vegas in 1879, introducing the revival styles that characterize the plaza today. The following decade brought changes that contributed to the current configuration of the plaza: a windmill which served as a gallows where a vigilance committee hanged criminals was removed owing to complaints from arriving railroad passengers, the Plaza Hotel was built and the "Great Emporium" of the Charles Ilfeld mercan-

tile company was constructed. The Plaza and the area around it formed an important commercial center from the founding of the town to the arrival of the railroad. After this important milestone, East Las Vegas, which formed along the railroad east of the Gallinas River, became the center of commercial activity. Since the 1980s many buildings on the Plaza and Bridge Street have been renovated, and the plaza again serves as the social, economic and political center of Las Vegas.

Las Vegas Railroad and Power Company Building
N. 12th St.
SR #437 (1976), NR #85002640 (1985), ⊠ 1715

Library Park Historic District
Library Park and vicinity
SR #325 (1974), NR #79001549 (1979), ⊠ 1715

Lincoln Park Historic District
Bounded by Douglas Ave., Grand Ave., Gallinas St. and Twelfth St.
SR #331 (1974), NR #79001550 (1979), NR #87001120 (1987), ⊠ 1715

Elisha V. Long House
903 7th St.
SR #438 (1976), NORTH NEW TOWN HISTORIC DISTRICT

Las Vegas Masonic Temple
518½ Douglas Ave.
SR #326 (1974), DOUGLAS/SIXTH STREET HISTORIC DISTRICT

2005 Montezuma
SR #1088 (1984), NR #85002655 (1985), ⊠ 1715

613 Mora
SR #1084 (1984), NR #85002650 (1985), ⊠ 1715

618 Mora
SR #1085 (1984), NR #85002651 (1985), ⊠ 1715

Murphy Drug Store
In Crockett Building, 600 Douglas Ave.
SR #455 (1976), DOUGLAS/SIXTH STREET HISTORIC DISTRICT

1202 Ninth Street
SR #1067 (1984), NR #85002632 (1985), ⊠ 1715

Patrick Nolan House
110 10th St.
SR #1053 (1984), NR #85002619 (1985), ⊠ 1715

North New Town Historic District
Bounded by National St., Friedman St., 3rd St., 8th St.
SR #892 (1982), NR #83001627 (1983)

Old Las Vegas City Hall
6th and University
SR #328 (1974), DOUGLAS/SIXTH STREET HISTORIC DISTRICT

Old Las Vegas Post Office
901 Douglas Ave.
SR #1035 (1984), NR #85002598 (1985), ⊠ 1715

Old Town Residential Historic District
Bounded by Perey St., Mills Ave., New Mexico Ave. and Gonzales St.
SR #895 (1982), NR #83004161 (1983)

2203 New Mexico Avenue
SR #1087 (1984), NR #85002654 (1985), ⊠ 1715

Our Lady of Sorrows Church
W. National Ave.
SR #318 (1974), NR #76001197 (1976), OLD TOWN RESIDENTIAL HISTORIC DISTRICT

521 S. Pacific

SR #1092 (1984), NR #85002659 (1985), ☒ 1715

921 S. Pacific

SR #1044 (1984), NR #85002608 (1985), ☒ 1715

800 Pecos

SR #1066 (1984), NR #85002633 (1985), ☒ 1715

Pimter/O'Neil Rooming House

313 Railroad Ave.

SR #1059 (1984), NR #85002627 (1985), ☒ 1715

Plaza Hotel

230 N. Plaza

SR #313 (1974), LAS VEGAS PLAZA HISTORIC DISTRICT, ☒ 1715

The Plaza Hotel, built on the Las Vegas Plaza in 1880, was one of the first of the buildings that transformed the Plaza after the railroad reached Las Vegas in 1879. The three-story, red brick hotel, with its ornate Victorian facade decorated with wrought iron and sculptured trim, was the leading hotel in Las Vegas, patronized by businessmen and ranchers and used for meetings, banquets and dances, until the Castañeda opened in East Las Vegas in 1899. The Plaza continued to be popular, however, and in the winter of 1913 was occupied by the Lubin Company as the headquarters for movie actor Romaine Fielding and his supporting cast while he filmed "The Golden God" and several other popular movies. The name "Hotel Romaine" was painted on the west wall of the hotel and is faded but still visible. In 1982, after many years of limited use, the hotel was fully restored and reopened to the public.

Presbyterian Mission Church

1413 Chavez St.

SR #296 (1973), NR #78001825 (1978), OLD TOWN RESIDENTIAL HISTORIC DISTRICT

931 Prince St.

SR #1054 (1984), NR #85002620 (1985), ☒ 1715

Railroad Avenue Historic District

Railroad Ave., between Douglas Ave. and Jackson Ave.

SR #344 (1974), NR #79001551 (1979), ☒ 1715

119 Railroad Ave.

SR #1057 (1984), NR #85002624 (1985), ☒ 1715

309 Railroad Ave.

SR #1060 (1984), NR #85002628 (1985), ☒ 1715

733 Railroad Ave.

SR #1061 (1984), NR #85002629 (1985), ☒ 1715

919 Railroad Ave.

SR #1062 (1984), NR #85002630 (1985), ☒ 1715

1025 Railroad Ave.

SR #1063 (1984), NR #85002631 (1985), ☒ 1715

Rogers Hall Administration Building (NMHU)

National Ave.

SR #918 (1982), NR #88001559 (1988), ☒ 1707

1406 Romero
SR #1089 (1984), NR #85002656 (1985), ☒ 1715

Canuto Romero House
Vicinity of Mills Ave.
SR #1074 (1984), ☒ 1715

Don Benigno Romero House
2003 Hot Springs Blvd.
SR #445 (1976), OLD TOWN RESIDENTIAL HISTORIC DISTRICT

Emanuel Rosenwald Building
S. Plaza
SR #618 (1978), LAS VEGAS PLAZA HISTORIC DISTRICT, ☒ 1715

Collections at the Rough Riders Museum
National St. and 4th St.
SR #264 (1972)

Vidal and Elisa Salazar House
824 Railroad Ave.
SR #1064 (1984), NR #85002637 (1985), ☒ 1715

1221 San Francisco St.
SR #1075 (1984), NR #85002644 (1985), ☒ 1715

San Geronimo Historic District
Off NM 283, San Geronimo
SR #795 (1981), NR #83004163 (1983)

Schmitt/Laemmle House
1106 Columbia Ave.
SR #1078 (1984), NR #85002639 (1985), ☒ 1715

913 Second St.
SR #1029 (1984), NR #85002597 (1985), ☒ 1715

915 Second St.
SR #1030 (1984), NR #85002596 (1985), ☒ 1715

919 Second St.
SR #1031 (1984), NR #85002595 (1985), ☒ 1715

Serna/Blanchard House
2203 N. Gonzales
SR #1048 (1984), NR #85002614 (1985), ☒ 1715

Shawn/Guerin House
140 Delgado
SR #1049 (1984), NR #85002615 (1985), ☒ 1715

St. Anthony's Hospital Annex
700 Friedman Ave.
SR #1034 (1984), NR #85002592 (1985), ☒ 1715

St. Paul's Memorial Episcopal Church and Guild Hall
714-716 National Ave.
SR #338 (1974), NR #76001198 (1976), NORTH NEW TOWN HISTORIC DISTRICT

M. M. Sundt House
1607 8th St.
SR #1070 (1984), NR #85002638 (1985), ☒ 1715

Taichert Warehouse and Taichert Building
623 12th St. and 1201 National
SR #439 (1976), NR #85002618 (1985), NR #85002616 (1985), ☒ 1715

2501 Taos Alley
SR #1086 (1984), NR #85002652 (1985), ☒ 1715

312 Tecolote
SR #1045 (1984), NR #85002609 (1985), ☒ 1715

1114 Tenth St.
SR #1082 (1984), NR #85002649 (1985), ☒ 1715

Truder Park
Bounded by 2nd St., Washington and Grand
SR #1093 (1984), NR #85002661 (1985), ☒ 1715

Trujillo/Gonzales House
935 New Mexico
SR #1046 (1984), NR #85002617 (1985), ☒ 1715

821 Twelfth St.
SR #1077 (1984), NR #85002643 (1985), ☒ 1715

933 Twelfth St.
SR #1076 (1984), NR #85002642 (1985), ☒ 1715

United Methodist Church
718 8th St.
SR #458 (1984), NORTH NEW TOWN HISTORIC DISTRICT

508 University Ave.
SR #1050 (1984), NR #85002611 (1985), ☒ 1715

514 University Ave.
SR #1051 (1984), NR #85002610 (1985), ☒ 1715

Women's Christian Temperance Union (W.C.T.U.) Fountain in Fountain Park
Lincoln and Grand Ave.
SR #333 (1978), DOUGLAS/SIXTH STREET HISTORIC DISTRICT

C.W.G. Ward House
1301 8th St.
SR #1033 (1984), NR #85002593 (1985), ☒ 1715

Ledoux *(Mora County)*

North Carmen Historic District
SR #1522 (1990), NR #90001058 (1990), ☒ 1521

Ledoux Rural Historic District
NM 94
SR #1523 (1990), NR #90001057 (1990), ☒ 1521

Logan *(Quay County)*

McFarland Brothers Bank
1st St. and Martinez St.
SR #481 (1976)

Shollenbarger Mercantile Building
SR #483 (1976)

Los Montoyas *(San Miguel County)*

Hatch's Ranch
SR #201 (1970)

Maxwell *(Colfax County)*

Maxwell Irrigation Project
SR #564 (1978)

Mills *(Harding County)*

Orchard Ranch
SR #149 (1970)

Montoya *(Quay County)*

Route 66, State Maintained: Palomas to Montoya (Ozark Trail)
SR #1577 (1993), NR #93001208 (1994), ☒ 1564

Montezuma *(San Miguel County)*

Ice Pond Site
NM 65
SR #473 (1976)

Las Vegas Irrigation Project Diversion Dam

SR #561 (1978)

Montezuma Hotel Complex

NM 65

SR #227 (1971), NR #74001203 (1974)

Montezuma Hot Springs has long been known for its healing water and mud. The springs were the site of a small bathhouse resort in the 1850s and of a Union hospital during the Civil War, but it was not feasible to attempt large-scale commercialization of the Montezuma region until the Santa Fe Railway reached nearby Las Vegas in 1879. In that year, Bostonian Alden Speare purchased 800 acres and founded the Las Vegas Hot Springs Company; the railroad soon controlled a majority of the stock. The first hotel at the hot springs was built in 1879. A succession of more and more opulent hotels followed to accommodate a growing resort business fueled by an 1881 railroad spur to Montezuma. The last and most expensive of these early hotels burned in 1884. Subsequently, a stone hotel with elaborate fire prevention systems was designed by the influential Chicago architecture firm of Burnham and Root; it was called the Montezuma Hotel, and it opened in 1885. Even with fire plugs and hose reels in every hall, a slate roof and mercurial fire alarms set to go off at 150 degrees, a fire broke out in the attic the next year and the building suffered substantial damage. The hotel was repaired and the final facility was a multi-storied, turreted, balconied building, still referred to locally as "the castle." The Montezuma Hotel complex includes the earlier 1880 "stone hotel," the 1885 Queen Anne Style Montezuma Hotel, the power house and the frame Victorian billiard hall. The hotel was popular in the 1890s when the railroad brought guests on excursion tickets from all over the country, but its popularity waned as resorts were established in the national parks. The Atchison, Topeka and Santa Fe Railroad began a new resort hotel, El Tovar at the Grand Canyon, and closed the Montezuma in 1903. The complex has been operated by various seminaries and colleges since the 1920s but the Montezuma Hotel itself is now vacant. The Montezuma is one of the few surviving Queen Anne hotels in the United States.

Peterson Dam

NM 665

SR #571 (1978)

Mora *(Mora County)*

Mora Historic District
NM 518
SR #1524 (1990), NR #90001056 (1990), ☒ 1521

La Cueva Historic District
NM 3 and NM21
SR #142 (1970), NR #73001144 (1973)

Daniel Cassidy House
SR #1529 (1990), NR #90001062 (1990), ☒ 1521

John Doherty House
NM 3 and NM 38
SR #730 (1979)

Garcia House
NM 518
SR #1525 (1990), NR #90001063 (1990), ☒ 1521

Gordon/Sanchez Mill
NM 518
SR #1528 (1990), NR #90001061 (1990), ☒ 1521

Jose Olguin Barn and Corral Complex
El Alto Road and NM 434
SR #1527 (1990), NR #90001060 (1990), ☒ 1521

St. Vrain's Mill
NM 3 and NM 38
SR #147 (1970), NR #73001143 (1973)

Mosquero *(Harding County)*

Church of the Immaculate Conception and Campo Santo
NM 39
SR #135 (1969)

Harding County Courthouse
Pine St.
SR #1268 (1986), NR #87000895 (1987), ☒ 1722

Nara Visa *(Quay County)*

Nara Visa School
US 54
SR #930 (1983), NR #83004151 (1983)

Ocate *(Mora County)*

Ocate Creek Crossing and the Santa Fe Trail
North of junction of NM 120 and the Mora Ranch Road
SR #1584 (1993), NR #94000329 (1994), ☒ 1582

J. P. Strong Store
NM 21 and NM 120
SR #484 (1976), NR #79001542 (1979)

Narciso Valdez House (Lorenzo Lopez House)
NM 120
SR #305 (1973), NR #80004484 (1980)

Pecos *(San Miguel County)*

Pecos Pueblo National Monument and Collections ▲
NM 63
SR #74 (1969), NR #66000485 (1966), NR #91000822 (1991)

In the A.D. 1300s and 1400s, the movement of population out of the Four Corners created very large centers of population in the Rio Grande Valley and adjacent areas, including such sites as Frijoles Canyon (Bandelier National Monument), Puye and Pecos Pueblo. Because the Pecos area lies in a corridor between the Rio Grande and the Plains, it became a nexus of a mutually beneficial trade that exchanged corn, pottery, obsidian and turquoise from the west for bison hides and meat from the east. The Pecos people reached the height of

their influence and prosperity around 1450 to 1550. They welcomed the explorer Coronado in 1540, and when colonizer Juan de Oñate arrived in 1598, he immediately assigned a friar to Pecos, then the richest and largest of all New Mexico's pueblos; four successive churches were subsequently constructed. Although the Rio Grande-Plains trade continued after the arrival of the Spanish, the colonists' demands on the pueblo for taxes and tribute and their competition for trade items disrupted the trade. In the 1700s and early 1800s the pueblo was decimated by disease, raids by nomadic Indians and the encroachment of Hispanic neighbors. By 1838, the population had dwindled to 27 people who left Pecos to live in the other Towa-speaking pueblo, Jemez. In the 1920s, archaeologist Alfred Kidder and others met at Pecos, by then a partly excavated pueblo and mission complex, to develop a unified archaeological nomenclature for the Southwest which is now known as the Pecos Classification. This important contribution to Southwestern anthropology added to Pecos Pueblo's significance as a site with a long history.

San Antonio de Padua Church and Collections
NM 63
SR #304 (1973), NR #78001826 (1978)

Valencia Ranch Archaeological/Historical District
SR #925 (1983), NR #84002975 (1984)

Puerto de Luna
(Guadalupe County)

Alexander Grzelachowski House and Store
NM 91
SR #176 (1970), NR #93000570 (1993)

Former Guadalupe County Courthouse in Puerto de Luna
South side of NM 91
SR #1264 (1986), ▲ 1722

Raton *(Colfax County)*

Raton Downtown Historic District
Bounded by Rio Grande, Clark, 1st St. and 3rd St.
SR #470 (1976), NR #77000923 (1977)

Carl's Electric Building
220 S. 1st St.
SR #488 (1977), RATON DOWNTOWN HISTORIC DISTRICT

Catskill Charcoal Ovens
SR #401 (1975), NR #78001813 (1978)

Clifton House Site (LA 98721)
SR #1585 (1993), NR #94000325 (1995), ☒ 1582

Colfax County Courthouse
3rd St. and Savage St.
SR #1273 (1986), NR #87000882 (1987), ☒ 1722

Columbian School
700 N. 2nd St.
SR #1624 (1996), NR #96000261 (1996), ☒ 1617

Cook's Hall
Cook Ave. and 1st St.
SR #489 (1977), RATON DOWNTOWN HISTORIC DISTRICT

Coors Building
Near State Highway
SR #461 (1976), RATON DOWNTOWN HISTORIC DISTRICT

Corner Bar and Raton Hotel
244 S. 1st St.
SR #490 (1977), RATON DOWNTOWN HISTORIC DISTRICT

Gardiner Coke Ovens
SR #552 (1978)

Coal was discovered in Dillon Canyon in 1881 by James T. Gardiner, a geologist for the Atchison, Topeka and Santa Fe Railroad. The following year, the railroad opened the Old Gardiner Mine, also known as the Blossburg Number 4, to extract the coal that was crucial for railroad operations in the era of the coal-fired steam locomotive. The Raton Coal and Coke Company

acquired the mine in 1896 and, over the next few years, built coke ovens to process the coal from mines in the hill directly west of the site. The Gardiner coke ovens are a long battery of red brick structures that stretch a quarter of a mile in three parallel rows, lining the rim of Dillon Canyon. The ovens are twelve feet in diameter and six feet high. During mining operations, they were filled with coal and charcoal, lighted and sealed with bricks. Two days later, the coke would be removed. This was the largest battery of coal-coke ovens in New Mexico. The mining camp of Gardiner grew up around these operations, and soon became a prosperous place. In the 1920s it was home to 400 people, a mercantile company, two churches, a hospital, a saloon and the buildings of the Raton Coal and Coke Company. The mines closed during the Great Depression, and the town was gradually abandoned.

Haven Hotel
S. 1st St.
SR #463 (1976), RATON DOWNTOWN HISTORIC DISTRICT

Investment Block
132 N. 1st St.
SR #493 (1977), RATON DOWNTOWN HISTORIC DISTRICT

Joseph Building
100 S. 1st St.
SR #465 (1976), RATON DOWNTOWN HISTORIC DISTRICT

Kearny School
800 S. 3rd St.
SR #1626 (1996), NR #96000259 (1996), ☒ 1617

Longfellow School
700 E. 4th St.
SR #1625 (1996), NR #96000262 (1996), ☒ 1617

New York and Golden Rule Stores
120-124 1st St.
SR #476 (1976), RATON DOWNTOWN HISTORIC DISTRICT

Palace Hotel
1st St. and Cook Ave.
SR #469 (1976), RATON DOWNTOWN HISTORIC DISTRICT

Raton Armory
901 S. 3rd St.
SR #1628 (1996), NR #96000260 (1996), ☒ 1617

Raton Junior/Senior High School
500 S. 3rd St.
SR #1627 (1996), NR #96000263 (1996), ☒ 1617

Raton Pass ▲
I-25
SR #20 (1968), NR #66000474 (1966)

Raton Pass has been an important artery of commerce for two hundred years. It was initially used as the route of the Santa Fe Trail, a trade route between Missouri and Santa Fe established in 1821. The following year, a shorter and lower, but waterless, route ("The Cimarron Cutoff") was established, and the steep, treacherous Raton Pass route became known as the "Mountain Route." Later, "Uncle Dick" Wootton obtained charters to build a toll road through Raton Pass. He cleared, graded and built a bridge so that the road would be suitable for wagon and stagecoach travel, but he charged $1.50 a wagon, at the time a price even steeper than the pass. In 1878, the pass was contested by two railroad companies as the best route through the Rocky Mountains. The Atchison, Topeka and Santa Fe Railroad laid claim to the pass when they initiated construction during the middle of the night to beat out the rival Denver and Rio Grande. The original railway tunnel, built in 1878-79, proved to be inadequate for the heavy traffic, and a second tunnel was built in 1908. This tunnel, at 2,790 feet long, it is the longest railway underground passage in New Mexico.

Raton Water Works
South slope of Bartlett Mesa
SR #572 (1978)

Fred Roth Building
132 1st St.
SR #494 (1977), RATON DOWNTOWN HISTORIC DISTRICT

Shuler Theater
133 N. 2nd St.
SR #170 (1970), RATON DOWNTOWN HISTORIC DISTRICT

Swastika Hotel
2nd St. and Cook St.
SR #792 (1980), RATON DOWNTOWN HISTORIC DISTRICT

St. John's Methodist Episcopal Church
NM 72
SR #373 (1975), NR #78001814 (1978)

Rayado *(Colfax County)*

Rayado Historic District
NM 21 at Philmont Scout Ranch
SR #587 (1978)

Maxwell/Abreu and North (Martinez) Houses
Northwest corner of NM 121 and Rayado Creek Rd.
SR #1548 (1993), NR #93000253 (1993), RAYADO HISTORIC DISTRICT, ^1547

The Rayado Ranch of Colfax County
NM 121
SR #1547 (1993), RAYADO HISTORIC DISTRICT, ⊠ 1547

Rociada *(San Miguel County)*

Pendaries Grist Mill
East of Lower Rociada
SR #569 (1978), NR #79001552 (1979)

Rowe *(San Miguel County)*

W.J. Jackson Cabin
SR #788 (1980)

San Jon *(Quay County)*

Route 66, Locally Maintained: Glenrio to San Jon (Ozark Trail)
SR #1578 (1993), NR #93001207 (1994), ⊠ 1564

Route 66, State Maintained: San Jon to Tucumcari (Ozark Trail)
SR #1675 (1997), NR #97001399 (1997), ⊠ 1564

San Jon Site (LA 6437)
NM 39
SR #145 (1970)

San Miguel *(San Miguel County)*

San Miguel del Vado Historic District
NM 3
SR #150 (1970), NR #72000809 (1972)

Santa Rosa *(Guadalupe County)*

Jesus M. Casaus House
628 3rd St.
SR #848 (1981), NR #82003324 (1982)

Colonias de San Jose Historic District
Colonias
SR #1177 (1985), NR #86002331 (1986), ⊠ 1176

Former Guadalupe County Courthouse in Santa Rosa
Northwest corner of S. 4th St. and Parker Ave.
SR #1265 (1986), NR #87000890 (1987), ⊠ 1722

Hidden Lake Pictographs (LA 16955)
SR #426 (1975)

La Capilla de Santa Rosa
900 S. 3rd St.
SR #177 (1970)

La Placita de Abajo District
Colonias
SR #1178 (1985), NR #86002338 (1986),
⊠ 1176

Julius J. Moise House
400 Capitan St.
SR #1110 (1984), NR #84000633 (1984)

Park Lake Historic District
Junction of Will Rogers Dr. and Lake Dr.
SR #1620 (1996), NR #96000267 (1996),
⊠ 1617, ⊠ 1564

Hispanic *pastores,* or shepherds, ran sheep in the Santa Rosa area as early as the 1820s, but the first Hispanic settler of Santa Rosa was probably Celso Baca, who is said to have come here in 1865 seeking a curative spring for his sick daughter. The springs that percolate through limestone karsts and bubble up through sandstone near the surface have always been important to the town's image. The Park Lake Historic District, built to take advantage of these natural springs, is a twenty-five acre property on the east side of Santa Rosa. It was constructed as a Works Progress Administration (WPA) project, part of Roosevelt's New Deal for federal relief, between 1934 and 1940. The goal of Park Lake's construction was to create local jobs and promote health and recreation; it has also contributed to Santa Rosa's efforts to bill itself as the "city of natural lakes." The site includes a stone storage building, terraces defined by stone retaining walls, masonry canals, man-made Park Lake and its swimming beach, landscaped groves and lawns, and a recreation area. After completion of these facilities, advertising urged tourists traveling Route 66 to stop and visit the park to picnic and swim in the spring-fed lake. The District also became the focus of local outdoor recreation. After years of neglect, the park was rehabilitated and incorporated into a larger municipal park known as the Park Lake/Blue Hole Recreation Complex.

Sapello *(San Miguel County)*

Los Alamos (Village) Ranch House Historic District
SR #1613 (1995)

Springer *(Colfax County)*

The Brown Hotel
302 Maxwell Ave.
SR #1647 (1996)

R. H. Cowan Livery Stable
125 Maxwell Ave.
SR #530 (1977), NR #79001538 (1979)

El Vado de las Piedras and the Santa Fe Trail (Rock Crossing of the Canadian River)
US 56 at the Canadian River
SR #1583 (1993), NR #94000327 (1994),
⊠ 1582

Former Colfax County Courthouse in Springer
614 Maxwell Ave.
SR #509 (1977), NR #87000883 (1987),
⊠ 1722

Melvin W. Mills House
509 1st St.
SR #191 (1970), NR #70000400 (1970)

Point of Rocks Historic District
Jones Well Rd.
SR #1586 (1993), NR #94000328 (1994),
☒ 1582

Tecolote *(San Miguel County)*

Santa Fe Trail: San Miguel County Trail Segments (Tecolote Creek Crossing)
SR #1587 (1993), NR #94000326 (1994),
☒ 1582

Terrero *(San Miguel County)*

Connell's Cabin
NM 63
SR #1531 (1990)

Pecos River Bridge at Terrero
NM 63 over the Pecos River
SR #1673 (1997), NR #97000739 (1997),
☒ 1661

Tucumcari *(Quay County)*

Metropolitan Park Bathhouse and Pool Historic District (Five-Mile Park)
I-40 South Frontage Rd.
SR #1618 (1996), NR #96000268 (1996),
☒ 1617

Arch Hurley Conservancy District Office Building (Tucumcari Project Office Building)
101 E. High St.
SR #1599, NR #94001403 (1994)

Blue Swallow Motel
815 E. Tucumcari Blvd.
SR #1575 (1993), NR #93001210 (1993),
☒ 1564

In the 1920s, America embraced the automobile, and US 66 emerged as a modern highway that linked Chicago with Los Angeles. Route 66 formed the Main Street of many towns along its path and was dotted with traveler services, a response to an increase in automobile tourism. The Blue Swallow Motel is one of the best remaining examples of an early tourist court motel along Route 66 in New Mexico. It was constructed in 1942 by W.A. Huggins, a Tucumcari carpenter, for rancher Ted Jones, and it consists of two one-story buildings: the L-shaped motel with a metal shed roof, pink stucco walls over hollow tile bricks, and a concrete foundation; and the office and manager's residence. The motel reflects the Southwest Vernacular Style, with its shell designs and stepped parapet. Most of the motel's signage dates to the 1950s. The parapet of the motel is outlined in neon with blue neon swallows. Each room has its own garage. The Blue Swallow, with its L-shaped plan, metal awnings, signage and use of

blue neon, is one of the best examples of a largely unaltered pre-war tourist court remaining along Route 66.

Montgomery House
401 S. 1st St.
SR #1692 (1997)

Quay County Courthouse
3rd St.
SR #1280 (1986), ⊠ 1722

Richardson's Store
Montoya by-pass, I-40
SR #525 (1977), NR #78001819 (1978)

Rock Island/Southern Pacific Passenger Depot
2nd St. and Railroad Ave.
SR #1512 (1989)

Valmora *(Mora County)*

Valmora Sanatorium Historic District
CR 97 and NM 161
SR #1545 (1992), NR #95000286 (1995)

Variadero *(San Miguel County)*

Variadero Bridge
NM 104 over the Rio Conchas
SR #1672 (1997), NR #97000736 (1997), ⊠ 1661

Wagon Mound *(Mora County)*

Farmers and Stockmens Bank
801 Nolan St.
SR #1610 (1995)

Santa Clara Hotel (Chamblis Hotel)
111 Railroad Ave.
SR #794 (1980), NR #91000602 (1991)

Wagon Mound ▲
SR #32 (1968), NR #66000478 (1966)

Wagon Mound and Santa Clara Canyon were two important natural features on the "Cimarron Cutoff" of the Santa Fe Trail from Missouri to New Mexico. Wagon Mound, the last great natural navigational landmark on westward journey to Santa Fe, let travelers know they were reaching settled New Mexico, 600 miles from their points of departure in Missouri. Early travelers thought the mesa resembled a shoe; a trader later named it the Wagon Mound, after its resemblance to a Conestoga wagon. The mesa, rising to about 7000 feet above sea level, was also a warning sign indicating possible Indian attacks. Santa Clara Canyon, two miles northwest of the Wagon Mound, offered wind-sheltered camping sites and a major water source; the water now serves the Berlier Ranch and the town of Wagon Mound. The Santa Fe Trail was one of America's first great trans-

continental roadways, linking Mexico and the United States during the Mexican Period (1821-1846) and continuing to be a vital trade and military connection from 1846, when the U.S. claimed New Mexico, to 1880, when the railroad reached the territory and the Trail was abandoned.

Watrous *(Mora County)*

Watrous (La Junta) ▲

SR #33 (1968), NR #66000480 (1966)

The Santa Fe Trail's "Mountain Branch," through Raton Pass, and "Cimarron Cutoff," through Wagon Mound, merged at the farming community of La Junta, at the juncture of the Mora and Sapello Rivers. The town of La Junta represented the first sign of civilization along the Cimarron Cutoff. When the railroad arrived in 1879, they laid out a town named Watrous for influential La Junta landowner Samuel B. Watrous, who donated land for the railroad right-of-way. The Watrous (La Junta) historic site includes the two Trail branches, the surviving buildings and sites associated with the Trail period (1821-1879) and the open rangeland that is the historical setting of the Trail. The branches of the Trail always had alternate alignments according to season, weather and convenience. These various routes of the two Trail branches spread out over the La Junta valley, joining and interconnecting in several places. Significant features of the historic site include the Fort Union corral; the Gregg Tavern-Stage Station, which operated as a stop on the Barlow-Sanderson Stage Line in the 1860s and 1870s; the William Tipton Store (owned by Watrous's son-in law); commercial structures and houses in Tiptonville; the Phoenix Ranch; the Samuel B. Watrous Ranch House and Store; the William Tipton Ranch Building; the Boné Cemetery;

and the Tiptonville Cemetery. In addition to these buildings which were a result of traffic on the Santa Fe Trail, trail ruts and wagon marks are still visible.

Fort Union National Monument
On NM 477

SR #61 (1969), NR #66000044 (1966)

William Kroenig Hay Barns No. 51 and 52

SR #903 (1982), ☒ 896

William Kroenig Hay Barns No. 53 and 54

SR #904 (1982), ☒ 896

William Kroenig Ranch Complex

SR #900 (1982), ☒ 896

La Junta Grist Mill

SR #905 (1982)

Loma Parda

SR #131 (1969)

Walter W. Lynam Ranch House

SR #902 (1982), ☒ 896

Enoch Tipton Ranch House

SR #898 (1982), ☒ 896

Martha Jane Tipton House

SR #899 (1982), ☒ 896

Joseph B. Watrous Ranch

SR #897 (1982), ☒ 896

Carl W. Wildenstein House (Glennwood Farm)

SR #901 (1982)

Central

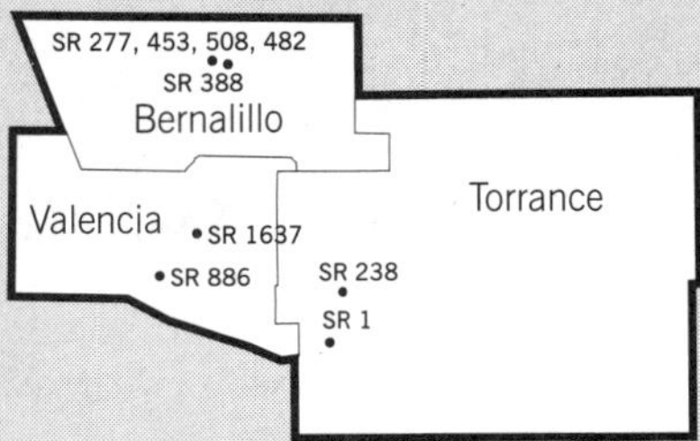

Although dominated by Albuquerque, the largest city in New Mexico, the Central region also comprises a varied landscape of forested mountains, vast plains dotted with saline lakes, and the Rio Grande Valley. Occupied prehistorically by pueblo-dwelling Indians, whose descendants still live along the Rio Grande, the central region was the scene of early Spanish exploration, the route of the Camino Real or Royal Road between the colony of Nuevo Mexico and the settlements of northern Mexico, and the location of some of the early plaza-centered Hispanic villages. With the arrival of the railroad in the 1880s Albuquerque began its pattern of ever-accelerating growth and dominance of commerce and politics in New Mexico, a pattern reinforced by its position at the crossroads of the state's major highways and railroads. The registered sites in the central region include large Colonial era missions and pueblos (long since abandoned owing to disease and attacks by nomadic tribes), a world class array of prehistoric rock carvings along the basalt escarpment west of Albuquerque, ancient Hispanic villages and pueblo settlements, the separate Colonial and railroad era towns of Albuquerque, and a wide variety of tourism, health-related, educational, and military sites.

Abo *(Torrance County)*

Abo Mission Ruin (LA 97) ▲

US 60

SR #1 (1968), NR #66000497 (1966)

As early as A.D. 1300, Pueblo Indians had established a settlement at Abo. Thirty-one years after Spanish colonizer Juan de Oñate visited it in 1598, Franciscan missionary Fray Francisco de Acevedo was assigned to Abo to establish a mission complex, San Gregorio de Abo. After fifteen years of drought, famine and Apache raids beginning about 1660, Abo was abandoned and its people joined pueblos along the Rio Grande. Abo Mission Ruin is now part of the Salinas Pueblo Missions National Monument, which also includes the separate sites of Quarai and Gran Quivira. Abo consists of extensive, unexcavated pueblo ruins and the excavated and stabilized ruins of the 17th century Franciscan mission complex.

Alameda *(Bernalillo County)*

Alameda School Site (LA 421)

Corrales Rd.

SR #1235 (1986), ☒ 1720

LA 717 (Puaray Pueblo—*possibly*)
11000 Block of Colt Ave.
SR #1243 (1986), ☒ 1720

Pueblo Calabacillas (LA 289)
South of intersection of Coors Rd. and Corrales Rd.
SR #1173 (1985)

North Edith Casa Corral (LA 50245)
Edith Blvd.
SR #1241 (2/28/86), ☒ 1720

Santa Rosalia de Corrales (LA 50268)
South of intersection of Coors Rd. and Corrales Rd.
SR #1174 (1985)

Albuquerque *(Bernalillo County)*

Agriculture Building, New Mexico State Fair
Main St. on the New Mexico State Fairgrounds
SR #1492 (1988)

Albuquerque Indian School Health Services #233
100 Menaul Blvd. NW
SR #844 (1981)

Albuquerque Municipal Airport Building
2920 Yale Blvd. SE
SR #482 (1976), NR #89000348 (1989)

From 1928, Albuquerque had been a stop for cross-country fliers, and city leaders believed that the city was destined to become the "air crossroads of the Southwest." They sought an airport to spur the economy and growth. The completion of Albuquerque's first airport building in 1939 capped a ten-year campaign to create a modern regional airport that would serve the growing city and the expanding transcontinental commercial airline industry. The Pueblo Revival style building was designed by City Architect Ernst L. Blumenthal and built by the Works Progress Administration (WPA), using adobe bricks and other local materials. It has an observation and air traffic control tower that is integrated into its terraced massing. Its lobby and other interior spaces, as well as its handcrafted tin-work chandeliers and southwestern furniture, create a romantic regional appearance. A new terminal two hundred yards to the east superseded this building in 1965. The original terminal is the only WPA airport built of adobe in the Pueblo Revival style.

Albuquerque Veterans Administration Medical Center Historic District
2100 Ridgecrest Dr. SE
SR #926 (1983), NR #83001614 (1983)

Gavino Anaya House
2939 Duranes Rd. NW
SR #933 (1983), NR #84002840 (1984), ☒ 1699

Juan Cristobal Armijo "New Homestead"
207 Griegos Rd. NE
SR #586 (1978), NR #82003309 (1982), ☒ 1699

Salvador Armijo House
618 Rio Grande Blvd. NW
SR #380 (1975), NR #76001191 (1976)

Art Annex (Old Library Building, UNM)
Northwest corner of Central Ave. and Terrace St.
SR #1497 (1988), NR #88001540 (1988), ☒ 1707

Art Annex (Old Chemistry Building/Craft Annex, UNM)
Northwest corner of Lomas Blvd. and University Ave.
SR #417 (1975), ☒ 1707

Atchison, Topeka & Santa Fe Railway Locomotive No. 2926
3rd St. and I-40
SR #366 (1975)

Atlantic & Pacific Railroad Superintendent's House
1023 S. 2nd St.
SR #398 (1975), NR #78001808 (1978)

Aztec Auto Court
3821 Central Ave. NE
SR #1571 (1993), NR #93001217 (1993), ☒ 1564

Barela/Bledsoe House
7017 Edith Blvd. NE
SR #462 (1976), NR #79001534 (1979), ☒ 1699

Adrian Barela House
7618 Guadalupe Trail NW
SR #940 (1983), NR #84002843 (1984), ☒ 1699

Barelas/South Fourth Street Historic District
Along 4th St. from Stover Ave. to Bridge St.
SR #1660 (1997), NR #97000774 (1997), ☒ 1687

Blythe House
1121-1123 8th St. NW
SR #710 (1979), ^1284

Boca Negra Cave Site (LA 46431)
SR #381 (1975)

Bond/Lovelace House
201 12th St. NW
SR #392 (1975)

Charles A. Bottger House
110 San Felipe NW
SR #751 (1979), NR #83001615 (1983)

Carlisle Gymnasium (UNM)
West of Yale Blvd.
SR #1453 (1988), NR #88001541 (1988), ☒ 1707

Chester Carnes House
701 13th St. NW
SR #729 (8/24/79), NR #80002529 (1980), ☒ 1284

Castle Apartments
1410 Central SW
SR #1213 (1985), NR#86000219 (1986)

Chamisal Site (LA 22765)
850 Chamisal Rd. NW
SR #779 (1980)

Champion Grocery Building
622-626 Tijeras NW
SR #521 (1977)

Kate Nichols Chaves House
501 11th St.
SR #522 (1977), FOURTH WARD HISTORIC DISTRICT, ☒ 1284

Juan Chavez House
7809 4th St., NW
SR #936 (1983), NR #84002849 (1984), ☒ 1699

Juan de Dios Chavez House
205 Griegos Rd. NW
SR #939 (1983), NR #84002847 (1984), ☒ 1699

Rumaldo Chavez House
10023 Edith Blvd. NE
SR #780 (1980), NR #80002530 (1980), ☒ 1699

C.H. Connor House
400 12th St.
SR #583 (1978), FOURTH WARD HISTORIC DISTRICT, ☒ 1284

Continental Oil Company Warehouse
1425 William SE
SR #1532 (1990)

J.H. Coons House
215 12th St.
SR #529 (1977)

Coronado School
601 4th St. SW
SR #1644 (1996), NR #96001383 (1996), ☒ 1617

Cottage Bakery (Spot Ice Cream Company)
2000 Central Ave. SE
SR #1567 (1993), NR #93001218 (1993), ☒ 1564

Davis House
704 Parkland Circle SE
SR #758 (1979), NR #80002531 (1980)

Robert Dietz Farmhouse
4117 Rio Grande Blvd. NW
SR #946 (1983), NR #84002852 (1984), ☒ 1699

Luciano Duran House
1805 ½ Lomas Blvd. NW
SR #523 (1977)

Eighth Street/Forrester District
Roughly bounded by Mountain Rd., Lomas Blvd., Forrester St. and 7th St.
SR #731 (1979), NR #80002532 (1980), ☒ 1284

El Campo Tourist Courts
5800 Central Ave. SW
SR #1588 (1993), NR #93001465 (1994), ☒ 1564

El Vado Auto Court
2500 Central Ave. SW
SR #1570 (1993), NR #93001214 (1993), ☒ 1564

Eller Apartments
113-127 8th St. SW
SR #951 (1983), NR #84002855 (1984)

Enchanted Mesa Trading Post
9612 Central Ave. SE
SR #1680 (1997), NR #97001595 (1998), ☒ 1564

Farwell/Simms House
211 14th St. NW
SR #659 (1978)

Federal Building - 1930
421 Gold Ave. SW
SR #700 (1978), NR #80002533 (1980)

Erna Fergusson House
1021 Orchard NW
SR #732 (1979)

The Fez Club
809 Copper NW
SR #531 (1977), FOURTH WARD HISTORIC DISTRICT, ☒ 1284

First Methodist Episcopal Church (Friendship Hall)
3rd St. and Lead Ave.
SR #383 (1975), NR #76001192 (1976)

First National Bank Building
217-233 Central Ave. NW
SR #660 (1978), NR #79003127 (1979)

F.M. Mercantile
1522 Edith Blvd.
SR #495 (1977)

Creighton Foraker Farmhouse
905 Menaul Blvd. NW
SR #945 (1983), NR #84002858 (1984), ☒ 1699

Fourth Ward Historic District
Roughly bounded by Central Ave., Lomas Blvd., 8th St. and 15th St.
SR #733 (1979), NR #80002534 (1980), ☒ 1284

J.A. Garcia House
908 Tijeras NW
SR #734 (1979), FOURTH WARD HISTORIC DISTRICT, ☒ 1284

Juan Antonio Garcia House
7442 Edith Blvd. NE
SR #471 (1976), NR #82003311 (1982), ☒ 1699

James N. Gladding House
643 Cedar St. NE
SR #759 (1979), NR #80002535 (1980)

Refugio Gomez House
7604 Guadalupe Trail NW
SR #941 (1983), NR #84002864 (1984), ☒ 1699

Apolonio Gonzales House
1524 Granite Ave. NW
SR #735 (1979)

Elias Gonzales House
821 12th St. NW
SR #736 (1979)

Good Shepherd Refuge
601 2nd St. SW
SR #393 (1975)

Charles Grande House
4317 Grande Ave. NW
SR #938 (1983), NR #84002866 (1984), ☒ 1699

Tomasa Griego de Garcia House
6939 Edith Blvd. NE
SR #466 (1976), NR #79001535 (1979), ☒ 1699

Grunsfeld/Hubbell House
909 Copper Ave. NW
SR #661 (1978), ^1284

Delfinia Gurule House
306 16th St. NW
SR #1285 (1979), NR #80002536 (1980), ☒ 1284

Harwood School
1114 7th St. NW
SR #737 (1979), NR #80002537 (1980), ☒ 1284

A. W. Hayden House
609 Marble NW
SR #753 (1979), NR #80002538 (1980), ☒ 1284

Hebenstreit House
200 Laguna Blvd. SW
SR #479 (1976)

Hesselden House
1211-1215 Roma NW
SR #496 (1977), ☒ 1284

Hilltop Lodge
5410 Central Ave. SW
SR #1679 (1997), NR #97001597 (1998), ☒ 1564, ☒ 1679

Hodgin Hall (UNM)
SW corner of University of New Mexico campus
SR #336 (1974), NR #78001803 (1978)

Hope Building
220 Gold Ave. SW
SR #768 (1980), NR #80002539 (1980)

Horn Oil Co. and Lodge
1720 Central Ave. SW
SR #1682 (1997), NR #97001591 (1998), ☒ 1564

Hudson House
817 Gold Ave. SW
SR #839 (1981), NR #82003313 (1982)

Huning Highlands Historic District
Bounded by Grand Ave., I-25, Iron Ave. and the Santa Fe railroad
SR #464 (1976), NR #78001804 (1978)

Indian Petroglyph State Park (LA 9054-9059)
Off Montano Rd.
SR #284 (1973)

Jones Motor Company
3226 Central Ave. SE
SR #1568 (1993), NR #93001219 (1993), ⊠ 1564

Thomas F. Keleher House
803 Tijeras NW
SR #738 (1979), ⊠ 1284

Thomas F. Keleher, Jr. House
312 Keleher St.
SR #739 (1979), ⊠ 1284

Kellogg/Elder House
314 Arno St.
SR #740 (1979)

Kelvinator House
324 Hermosa Dr. SE
SR #704 (1978)

KiMo Theater
421 Central Ave.
SR #453 (1976), NR #77000920 (1977)

In 1926, Oreste Bachechi, the owner of Albuquerque's Pastime Theater, hired Los Angeles architect Carl Boller, who specialized in theatrical architecture, to design the KiMo for both movies and stage productions. The theater opened in 1927 during the period of the great movie palaces. Pablo Abeita, Governor of Isleta Pueblo, suggested the name *kimo* meaning "mountain lion" in Tiwa. The KiMo Theater is a

steel frame, brick and masonry building of three stories, with a five-story fly loft for raising scenery and a seating capacity of 1300. The exterior is finished with light brown stucco, with ornamental details of glazed terra-cotta tile. Exterior tile and reliefs set an American Indian theme that is carried out in greater detail in the building's interior. Decorative elements include longhorn skulls with electric light eyes, and painted American Indian motifs including suns, birds and swastikas border the proscenium arch. The large *vigas* are also covered with Indian motifs. The ceiling decorations include Navajo *Yei* figures, buffalo, lightning and sun symbols. Large quadratura murals on the upper walls of the lobby depict the legendary Seven Cities of Cíbola sought by early Spanish explorers. The KiMo is a fine regional example of a "movie palace," a new building type created by the rise of the movie industry.

S. H. Kress Building
414-416 Central Ave. SW
SR #1004 (1984), NR #84002871 (1984)

Kromer House
1024 El Pueblo Rd. NW
SR #781 (1980), NR #82001048 (1982), ⊠ 1699

La Luz de Oeste (Units 1, 2, and 3)
Coors Blvd. NW between Western Trail and Montano Rd.
SR #539 (1977)

La Mesa Motel
7407 Central Ave. NE
SR #1569 (1993), NR #93001220 (1993), ☒ 1564

La Puerta Lodge
9710 Central Ave. SE
SR #1681 (1997), NR #97001596 (1998), ☒ 1564

La Quinta
4803 Rio Grande Blvd. NW
SR #394 (1975)

Las Imagines: Albuquerque West Mesa Archaeological District
SR #1234 (1986), NR #86003142 (1986)

Charles LeFeber House
313 15th St. NW
SR #741 (1979), NR #80002540 (1980), ☒ 1284

Lembke House
312 Laguna SW
SR #467 (1976), NR #80002541 (1980)

William J. Leverett House
301 Dartmouth NE
SR #1212 (1985), NR #86000221 (1986)

Charles W. Lewis Building
1405-1407 2nd St. SW
SR #711 (1979), NR #79001533 (1979)

Linder House
915 Ridgecrest Dr. SE
SR #1536 (1991)

Hilario Lopez House
208 16th St. NW
SR #1286 (1979), NR #80002542 (1980), ☒ 1284

Los Candelarias Chapel (San Antonio Chapel)
1934 Candelaria NW
SR #932 (1983), NR #84002844 (1984), ☒ 1699

Los Duranes Chapel
2601 Indian School Rd. NW
SR #948 (1983), NR #84002854 (1984), ☒ 1699

Los Griegos Historic District
Griegos Rd. and Rio Grande Blvd.
SR #931 (1983), NR #84002874 (1984), ☒ 1699

Los Poblanos Historic District
Bounded by Rio Grande Pl., Griegos Lateral, Riverside Drain and Rio Grande Blvd.
SR #853 (1982), NR #82003321 (1982), ☒ 1699, ☒ 1703

Los Ranchos Archaeological District
Rio Grande Blvd. between Corrales Rd. and Montano Rd.
SR #1281 (1986)

Los Tomases Chapel
3101 Los Tomases Dr. NW
SR #944 (1983), NR #84002876 (1984), ☒ 1699

Francisco Lucero y Montoya House
9742 4th St. NW
SR #937 (1983), NR #84002880 (1984), ☒ 1699

Maisel's Indian Trading Post
510 Central Ave. SW
SR #1565 (1993), NR #93001215 (1993), ☒ 1564

Henry Mann House
723 14th St. NW
SR #742 (1979), NR #80002543 (1980), ☒ 1284

Manzano Day School (La Glorieta)
1801 Central Ave. NW
SR #70 (1969), NR #83001616 (1983),
⊠ 1284

Marchant House
1322 Mountain Rd. NW
SR #754 (1979)

Matthews/Dornacker House
1701 Las Lomas Rd. NE
SR #1634 (1996)

Collections at the Maxwell Museum (UNM)
Fine Arts Dept. and Maxwell Museum
SR #215 (1971)

Harry W. McAvoy House
1401 Las Lomas Rd.
SR #762 (1979), SPRUCE PARK HISTORIC DISTRICT

McCanna/Hubbell Building (Albuquerque Gas & Electric Company Building)
418-424 Central SW
SR #829 (1981), NR #82003314 (1982)

McQuade House
201 Walter NE
SR #755 (1979), HUNING HIGHLANDS HISTORIC DISTRICT

Louis A. McRae House
601 Marble Ave. NW
SR #337 (1974)

Menaul School Historic District
Bounded by Broadway, Claremont and Menaul Blvd.
SR #420 (1975), NR #83001617 (1983),
⊠ 1699

John Milne House
804 Park Ave. SW
SR #1172 (1985), NR #86000223 (1986)

Modern Auto Court
3712 Central Ave. SE
SR #1572 (1993), NR #93001221 (1993),
⊠ 1564

Monte Vista Fire Station
3201 Central Ave. NE
SR #849 (1981), NR #87001121 (1987)

Monte Vista School
3211 Monte Vista Blvd. NE
SR #830 (1981), NR #81000399 (1981)

National Humane Alliance Animal Fountain (Ensign Fountain)
615 Virginia Ave. SE
SR #1192 (1985), NR #86003120 (1986)

New Mexico/Arizona Wool Warehouse
520 1st St. NW
SR #787 (1980), NR #81000400 (1981)

Nob Hill Business Center
3500 Central Ave. SE
SR #991 (1983), NR #84004143 (1994)

Robert Nordhaus House
6900 Rio Grande Blvd. NW
SR #942 (1983), NR #84002883 (1984),
⊠ 1699

Occidental Insurance Company Building
119 3rd St. SW
SR #277 (1973), NR #78001805 (1978)

The Occidental Life Insurance Company was founded in Albuquerque in 1906. The company built this, their second headquarters facility, in 1917. Architect Henry Trost

of the El Paso architecture firm of Trost and Trost, designers of many New Mexico buildings, modeled the building on the Doge's Palace in Venice, supposedly at the suggestion of Occidental's president, who had just toured Europe. Trost designed the building with an overhanging cornice and nine-foot deep porches on the south and east, and finished the interior in mahogany and Circassian walnut. The sheathing of glazed white terra-cotta tile was manufactured by the Denver Terra-Cotta Tile company. Pointed Venetian Gothic arches, capped by a row of quatrefoils, range down the street facades. Much of the tile forms interlocking floral patterns. A fire in 1933 destroyed the roof and interior; the 1934 rebuilding, designed by Albuquerque architect Miles Britelle, made the roof edge more closely resemble that of the Doge's Palace. The roof of the building is supported by steel columns which has permitted flexibility in the interior; this foresight has allowed the building's continued use. In 1981, a two-story office building was built within the original walls. A similar building in Oklahoma City was demolished in 1972, and now the Occidental Life Insurance Building is unique in the United States.

Oestriech House
1013 8th St. NW
SR #663 (1978)

Ohlrau House
818-820 Arno SE
SR #770 (1980)

J. H. O'Rielly House
220 9th St. NW
SR #534 (1977), NR #79C03442 (1979)

Old Albuquerque High School
Central and Broadway SE
SR #508 (1977), HUNING HIGHLANDS HISTORIC DISTRICT

Albuquerque's first public high school was designed by the El Paso architecture firm of Trost and Trost, architects responsible for many public buildings in the Southwest, and was completed in 1914. This original building is called Old Main; it faces Central Avenue and is of the Gothic Revival style then prevalent for schools, with brick and white trim. The imposing building contained the latest innovations in school design and equipment, including a science laboratory, a gymnasium, a library, classrooms, an 850-seat auditorium, steel lockers and a master clock and bell system. It served up to 500 students each year, but enrollment quickly increased, and more buildings were needed. In 1927, local architect George Williamson designed a Manual Arts building in similar style. Ten years later, between 1937 and 1940, Albuquerque Public Schools used New Deal funding to add the Classroom Building, the Gymnasium Building and the Library Building. All three were designed by local architect Louis Hesselden to follow the Gothic Revival style of the first two buildings. The five buildings form a compact campus around a central courtyard. Old Albuquerque High School was the city's only high school from 1914 to 1948, when,

after World War II, Albuquerque was growing so quickly that a second high school was built. Until the 1980s the Old High School was still used for school programs; it now lies vacant, awaiting a new use.

Old Albuquerque Historic District
SR #749 (1979)

Old Albuquerque Public Library
423 Central NE
SR #395 (1975), HUNING HIGHLANDS HISTORIC DISTRICT

Old Armijo School
1021 Isleta Blvd. SE
SR #852 (1982), NR #82003315 (1982)

Old Hilton Hotel
125 2nd St. NW
SR #992 (1983), NR #84002868 (1984)

Old Post Office
123 4th St. SW
SR #706 (1978), NR #80002544 (1980)

Orilla de la Acequia Historic District
Vicinity of Lomas and Central, east of Old Town
SR #756 (1979)

Our Lady of Mt. Carmel Church (Ranchos Chapel)
7813 Edith Blvd. NE
SR #414 (1975), NR #84002884 (1984), LOS GRIEGOS HISTORIC DISTRICT, ^1699

Our Lady of the Angels School
320 Romero St. NW
SR #1025 (1984), NR #84000426 (1984), OLD ALBUQUERQUE HISTORIC DISTRICT

Pacific Desk Building
213-215 Gold Ave. SW
SR #772 (1980), NR #80002545 (1980)

John Pearce House
718 Central Ave. SW
SR #782 (1980), NR #80002546 (1980)

Pi Kappa Alpha Estufa (UNM)
Corner of University Blvd. and Grand Ave. (now Martin Luther King Blvd.)
SR #1412 (1988), NR #88001542 (1988), ☒ 1707

Piedras Marcadas Pueblo (Mann Site) (LA 290)
SR #1175 (1985), NR #90000160 (1990)

Pig 'n Calf Lunch (University Cafe)
2106 Central Ave. SE
SR #1566 (1993), NR #93001222 (1994), ☒ 1564

President's House (UNM)
NE corner of Roma Ave. and Yale Blvd.
SR #1454 (1988), NR #88001543 (1988), ☒ 1707

Puccini Building
620-624 Central Ave. SW
SR #757 (1979)

Ernie Pyle House
900 Girard Blvd. SE
SR #1659 (1997), NR #97001103 (1997)

Rancho de Carnue (LA 12315-12316)
SR #396 (1976), NR #77000921 (1977)

Sara Raynolds Hall (UNM)
Terrace St. north of Central Ave.
SR #1455 (1988), NR #88001544 (1988), ☒ 1707

Rio Puerco Bridge
I-40 over the Rio Puerco
SR #1662 (1997), NR #97000735 1997), ☒ 1661

Robertson House
303 12th St. NW
SR #519 (1977)

701 Roma NW
SR #1127 (1985), NR #85000375 (1985)

Felipe Romero House
7522 Edith Blvd. NE
SR #935 (1983), NR #84002885 (1984),
☒ 1699

Roosevelt Park (Terrace Park)
Coal Ave. and Spruce Ave. SE
SR #1646 (1996), NR #96C01384 (1996),
☒ 1617

Rosenwald Building
320 Central Ave. SW
SR #588 (1978), NR #78001806 (1978)

Route 66, State Maintained from Albuquerque to Rio Puerco (Aguna Cutoff)
SR #1674 (1997), NR #97001396 (1997),
☒ 1564

J.E. Saint House
216 9th St. NW
SR #745 (1979), FOURTH WARD DISTRICT, ☒ 1284

Sais House
214 San Pasquale NW
SR #1635 (1996)

San Felipe de Neri Church
North side of Old Town Plaza
SR #39 (1976), NR #69000140 (1969), OLD ALBUQUERQUE HISTORIC DISTRICT

San Ignacio Church
1300 Walter St. NE
SR #520 (1977), NR #79001536 (1979)

Manuel Sanchez y Aranda House
409 47th St. NW
SR #1282 (1986)

Santa Barbara School
1420 Edith Blvd. NE
SR #1510 (1989), NR #89001590 (1989)

Scholes Hall (UNM)
Roma Ave. NE
SR #388 (1975), NR #88001545 (1988),
☒ 1707

Scholes Hall, built in 1934 to house classrooms, was the first major work at the University of New Mexico by noted New Mexican architect John Gaw Meem. His expertise was Pueblo Revival Style, a style utilized to complement other buildings on campus. The church of San Estéban Rey at Acoma Pueblo was used as a model for the I-shaped building. Features include two-story east and west wings and a recessed three-story central block with bell towers, a flat roof with exposed exterior vigas, hand-carved balconies and precast concrete spandrels. Its slightly recessed double-hung wood windows have concrete sills. North and south entries on both east and west wings have double leaf wood doors; the

south entrance in the central block has solid wood raised panel doors. Scholes Hall, central to the history of the University (founded in 1889) was constructed using labor and funding from the Works Progress Administration (WPA), a New Deal agency. Over the years, the building has undergone many changes, but it has continued to be used as a university building. It is now at the heart of the campus, housing administration, finance, admissions, registration and records.

Second United Presbyterian Church
812 Edith Blvd. NE
SR #1024 (1984), NR #84000563 (1984)

Samuel Shalit House
5209 4th St. NW
SR #947 (1983), NR #84002888 (1984),
☒ 1699

Shoup Boarding House
707 1st St. SW
SR #791 (1980), NR #83001618 (1983)

Silver Hill Historic District
Bounded by Gold Ave., Yale Blvd.,
Lead Ave., and Sycamore St.
SR #1254 (1986), NR #86002414 (1986)

Simms/Anderman House
415 11th St. NW
SR #526 (1977), ☒ 1284

Simms Building
400 Gold Ave. SW
SR #1693 (1997), NR #97001653 (1998)

John F. Simms House
4317 Rio Grande Blvd. NW
SR #771 (1980), LOS POBLANOS HISTORIC DISTRICT

Skinner Building
722-724 Central Ave. SW
SR #784 (1980), NR #80004485 (1980)

Solar Building
213 Truman St. NE
SR #1171 (1985), NR #89001589 (1989)\

Southwestern Brewery and Ice Company
601 Commercial NE
SR #397 (1975), NR #78001807 (1978)

Berthold Spitz House
323 N. 10th St.
SR #371 (1975), NR #77000922 (1977), FOURTH WARD HISTORIC DISTRICT,
☒ 1284

Springer Building
121 Tijeras Ave. NE
SR #785 (1980), NR #80002547 (1980)

Spruce Park Historic District
Bounded by University Blvd.,
Grand Ave., Las Lomas Rd. and Cedar St.
SR #798 (1982), NR #82003317 (1982)

St. Joseph 1930 Hospital
715 Grand Ave. NE
SR #854 (1982), NR #82003316 (1982)

Mary Strong House
802 Silver Ave. SE
SR #510 (1977)

Sunshine Building
120 Central Ave. SW
SR #1170 (1985)

Domingo Tafoya House
10021 Edith Blvd. NE
SR #786 (1980), NR #80002528 (1980),
☒ 1699

Tower Courts
2210 Central Ave. SW
SR #1573 (1993), NR #93001216 (1993),
☒ 1564

Antonio Vigil House
413 Romero St.
SR #459 (1976), NR #78001809 (1978)

Washington Apartments
1002-1008 Central Ave. SW
SR #589 (1978), NR #82003319 (1982)

Watson Historic District
16th St. and 17th St. between Lomas Blvd. and Mountain Rd.
SR #747 (1979), ⊠ 1284

Watson House
606 17th St. NW
SR #460 (1976)

Lettie Watson House
316 Walter SE
SR #748 (1979)

H.B. Weiller House
1228 Central Ave. SW
SR #799 (1981)

Werner/Gilchrist House
202 Cornell SE
SR #880 (1982), NR #82003320 (1982)

West San Jose School
1701 4th St. SW
SR #1645 (1996), NR #96001385 (1996), ⊠ 1617

Whittlesey House
201 Highland Park Cir. SE
SR #391 (1975)

J.W. Wilson House
202 High St. SE
SR #836 (1981)

W.H. Woolston House
1513 Las Lomas Rd. NE
SR #800 (1981), SPRUCE PARK HISTORIC DISTRICT

Yott House
3541 12th St. NW
SR #419 (1975)

Yrisarri Block (Stern Block)
400-402 Central Ave. SW
SR #1639 (1996)

Charles Zeiger House
3200 Edith Blvd. NE
SR #934 (1983), NR #84002889 (1984), ⊠ 1699

Belen *(Valencia County)*

Belen Harvey House
104 N. 1st St.
SR #886 (1982), NR #83004180 (1983)

The Santa Fe Hotel was built in 1901 as a simple two-story T-shaped brick structure with a pitched cross-gable roof. An extensive remodeling in 1910 by Santa Fe

Railway architect Myron Church transformed the trackside hotel into the Belen Harvey House, a Harvey House restaurant that served passengers on the Santa Fe and housed the Harvey Girl waitresses. The original roof was covered with red clay tile, and a flat-roofed wrap-around horseshoe arch portal was poured in place to provide the distinctive mission appearance. The building included both a simple lunchroom and a first class dining room with an extensive menu, fine linens, crystal and silver. It served as a Harvey House from 1910 to 1939. Until about 1939, it was the most visible and successful public building in Belen, a Spanish colonial town that became a major rail center at the crossroads of two routes. The building's Mission Revival style is an excellent example of the buildings built by the Atchison, Topeka and Santa Fe Railroad in New Mexico and the Southwest.

Belen Hotel
200 Becker Ave.
SR #774 (1980), NR #80002574 (1980)

Felipe Chaves House
325 Lala St.
SR #766 (1980), NR #80002575 (1980)

Old Jarales Schoolhouse
400 block, Jarales Rd.
SR #1594 (1994)

Pueblo Los Trujillos (LA 50271)
SR #1246 (1986), ☒ 1720

Bosque Farms *(Valencia County)*

Bosque Cooperative Building
1335 W. Bosque Loop
SR #1632 (1996)

Dust Bowl Home
930 S. Bosque Loop
SR #1409 (1988)

Cedar Crest *(Bernalillo County)*

San Antonio de Padua de Carnue (LA 24)
NM 14
SR #415 (1975)

Cedarvale *(Torrance County)*

Pueblo Colorado (South) (LA 476)
FR 458
SR #108 (1969)

Tabira Ruin (Pueblo Blanco South) (LA 51)
FR 533
SR #122 (1969)

Estancia *(Torrance County)*

Berkshire Hotel
SR #427 (1976)

Laguna *(Valencia County)*

SEE ALSO NORTHWESTERN REGION

Route 66: Correo to Laguna (National Old Trails Highway)
SR #1686 (1997), ☒ 1564

Los Lentes *(Valencia County)*

Be-jui Tu-ay (Rainbow Village) (LA 81)
SR #1236 (1986), ☒ 1720

Los Lentes Pueblo (LA 951)
SR #1240 (1986), ☒ 1720

Los Lunas *(Valencia County)*

Atchison, Topeka & Santa Fe Railroad Depot
US 85
SR #616 (1978), NR #79001562 (1979)

Huning Mercantile and House
Main St. and Los Lentes
SR #130 (1969)

Tranquilino Luna-Otero House
US 85 and NM 6
SR #283 (1973), NR #75001175 (1975)

Pottery Mound (LA 416)
SR #724 (1979)

Paia Romero Cafe
120 Main St. NW
SR #1648 (1996)

Dr. William Frederick Wittwer House
Main St.
SR #1128 (1985), NR #87000131 (1987)

Los Padillas *(Bernalillo County)*

Hubbell House
6029 Isleta Blvd. SW
SR #480 (1976)

Pure-e Tu-ay (LA 489)
SR #1248 (1986), ⊠ 1720

Moriarty *(Torrance County)*

Moriarty Eclipse Windmill
Off NM 222
SR #565 (1978), NR #79001561 (1979)

Greene Evans Garage (Jr.'s Tire Shop)
Broadway and Rte. 66
SR #1574 (1993), NR #93001211 (1993), ⊠ 1564

Mountainair *(Torrance County)*

Atchison, Topeka & Santa Fe Railway Depot
SR #349 (1974)

Mountainair Municipal Auditorium
Roosevelt Ave. and Beal St.
SR #1371 (1987), NR #87000651 (1987)

Rancho Bonito (LA 17117)
Gran Quivera Rd.
SR #514 (1977), NR #78001834 (1978)

Shaffer Hotel
Broadway St.
SR #517 (1977), NR #78003077 (1978)

Peralta *(Valencia County)*

Our Lady of Guadalupe Catholic Church
SR #477 (1976)

Pueblo of Isleta *(Bernalillo County)*

Pueblo of Isleta
SR #247 (1972), NR #75001162 (1975)

Punta *(Torrance County)*

Quarai Ruin (LA 3544, LA 95) ▲
SR #238 (1972), NR #66000498 (1966)

Quarai consists of a small 17th century church, a major 17th century Franciscan mission and church, and the remnants of a pueblo, in which several relatively small areas have been excavated. Like Abo and Gran Quivira, Quarai is a unit is of the Salinas Pueblo Missions National Monument. Some time in the A.D. 1100s, Tiwa-speaking Anasazi people from the Rio Grande Valley to the northwest and Piro-speaking Anasazi people from the Rio

Grande Valley to the west moved into the Salinas area. The first occupation of Quarai dates from around 1250, and around 1300 the first major structures were built in a number of the region's pueblos. In the 16th century, the Spanish arrived and established a mission at Quarai in 1630; designed by Juan Gutiérrez de la Chica in 1626, it included a *convento* and a church, Nuestra Señora de la Purisima Concepción de Cuarac. *Cuarac* was the 17th century Spanish spelling of Quarai. The pueblo was the headquarters of the Holy Office of the Inquisition in New Mexico and played a prominent role in the conflict between ecclesiastical and secular authorities in the 1600s. After years of drought, famine and Apache raids beginning about 1660, Quarai was abandoned like the other Salinas area pueblos. The people joined pueblos along the Rio Grande. During the 1700s and 1800s, Quarai was used occasionally as a base for military operations against Apaches.

San Antonito *(Bernalillo County)*

Paako Ruin (San Pedro Viejo) (LA 162)
SR #1378 (1987)

San Antonito Church and Cemetery
NM 14 and NM 536
SR #1643 (1996), NR #96001607 (1997), ☒ 1615

Tijeras *(Bernalillo County)*

Old Holy Child Tijeras Church
Tijeras Ave.
SR #511 (1977), NR #78001810 (1978)

Plaza de San Miguel de Carnue (LA 12924)
SR #422 (1975)

Silva Site (LA 12924)
SR #1250 (1986), ☒ 1720

Tijeras Pueblo Site (Cedro Canyon Site) (LA 581)
SR 14
SR #1494 (1989)

Tome *(Valencia County)*

Miguel E. Baca House
NM 47
SR #335 (1974), NR #78001835 (1978)

Comanche Springs Archaeological District (Los Ojuelos) (LA 14904)
SR #478 (1976), NR #87002080 (1987)

El Cerro Tomé (Tome Hill) (LA 8771, LA 50238, LA 108472)
SR #1637 (1996), NR #96000739 (1996)

El Cerro Tomé, or Tomé Hill, is a four-hundred foot high volcanic plug located on the northern boundary of the former Tomé Grant. There are three archaeological sites containing numerous prehistoric and historic petroglyphs, possible Pueblo shrines and Pueblo habitation sites on the hill. The main trails climbing the hill are marked with rocks and concrete slabs bearing religious paintings and phrases. At the summit are a Catholic shrine and four crosses, a *calvario* or destination for Catholic religious pilgrimages. These prehistoric and historic resources cover a period of about five thousand years, from late Archaic times

to the present. Most of the petroglyphs date from about A.D. 700 to about 1600. After Juan de Oñate established the first permanent Hispanic colony in New Mexico in 1598, the site was visited continuously by travelers on the Camino Real, the road that linked New Mexico with Mexico City, which skirted the hill. The Penitentes, a New Mexico religious society, was important in Tomé in the 19th century. This organization annually re-enacted Christ's carrying of the cross and held Good Friday services on Tomé Hill's summit. The hill is still regularly visited by pilgrims, particularly at Easter; it continues to play a role in the spiritual life of the Pueblo and Hispanic communities in the area.

Our Lady of the Immaculate Conception Church
NM 47
SR #73 (1969)

Tome Jail
Tome Plaza
SR #257 (1972), NR #77000932 (1977)

Turn *(Valencia County)*

Pueblo Casa Colorado (LA 50249)
NM 47
SR #1244 (1986), ⊠ 1720

Valencia *(Valencia County)*

Valencia Church
SR #887 (1982)

Valencia Pueblo (LA 953)
NM 47
SR #1252 (1986), ⊠ 1720

Veguita *(Valencia County)*

Casa Colorado del Sur (LA 779)
SR #1239 (1986), ⊠ 1720

Southwest

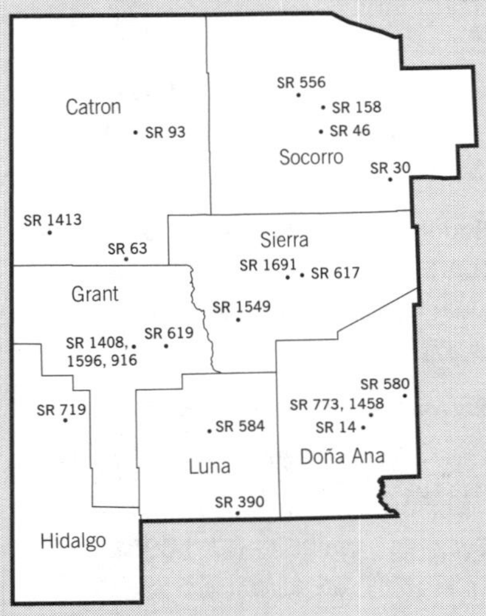

Southwestern New Mexico is a dramatic region of arid mountain ranges and vast waterless deserts with a rugged beauty all its own. From the stark, pure white landscape of White Sands National Monument to the jagged, unearthly peaks of the Organ Mountains; from the fertile and verdant floodplain of the Rio Grande to the trackless wastes of the *Jornada del Muerto;* from the bleak and arid Oscura, San Andres, and Jarilla Mountains to the rugged, heavily timbered Mimbres, Mogollon, and Black Range, and from the Plains of San Agustin in the north to the vast desert basins running down into Mexico in the south, the southwestern region has a history as varied as its landscape. Prehistorically this land was home to the Mogollon people, agriculturalists who adapted successfully to many environments, but perhaps none as successfully as those who lived in large pueblos along and near the Mimbres River. The people made pottery of such breathtaking loveliness that the greedy search for it has nearly caused the eradication of the archaeological record they left behind. Historically, the southwestern region was home to bands of Apache people — the Mescaleros, the Warm Spring, and most notably the Chiricahua, who it took the full might of the U.S. Army to subdue. The Rio Grande Valley was settled by Hispanic farmers, the desert basins by cattlemen, and the high country was and is home to those who took copper and silver and other precious metals from the earth. Registered sites here include the ruins of Mimbres pueblos, mining related ghost towns and near ghost towns, old Hispanic villages, the charming Victorian town of Silver City, ranching sites, and military sites associated with the Civil War, the Indian Wars, Pancho Villa's raid on the U.S., the Cold War, and even the Trinity Site — the National Historic Landmark where the first atomic bomb was tested in 1945.

Animas *(Hidalgo County)*

Alamo Hueco Ruin (LA 54053)
SR #1329 (1986), NR #92001800 (1993),
⊠ 1719

Box Canyon Site (LA 4980)
SR #1309 (1986), NR #92001796 (1993),
⊠ 1719

Brushy Creek Ruin (LA 54051)
SR #1328 (1986), NR #92001815 (1993),
⊠ 1719

Clanton Draw Site (LA 4979)
SR #1308 (1986), NR #92001795 (1993),
⊠ 1719

Cloverdale Park Site (LA 54034)
SR #1320 (1986), ⊠ 1719

Culberson Ruin (LA 31050)
SR #1312 (1986), NR #92001799 (1993),

☒ 1719

Double Adobe Creek Site (LA 54033)
SR #1319 (1986), NR #92001807 (1993),
☒ 1719

Hoskins Site (LA 54028)
SR #1316 (1986), NR #92001804 (1993),
☒ 1719

Joyce Well Site (LA 11823)
SR #1311 (1986), NR #92001798 (1993),
☒ 1719

LA 593
SR #1306 (1986), ☒ 1719

LA 54021
SR #1314 (1986), NR #92001802 (1993),
☒ 1719

LA 54036
SR #1321 (1986), ☒ 1719

LA 54042
SR #1324 (1986), NR #92001811 (1993),
☒ 1719

LA 54049
SR #1326 (1986), NR #92001813 (1993),
☒ 1719

LA 54050
SR #1327 (1986), NR #92001814 (1993),
☒ 1719

Little Site (LA 54029)
SR #1317 (1986), NR #92001805 (1993),
☒ 1719

Lunch Box Site (LA 54020)
SR #1313 (1986), NR #92001801 (1993),
☒ 1719

Maddox Ranch Site (LA 498)
NM 338
SR #1305 (1986), NR #92001793 (1993),
☒ 1719

Metate Ruin (LA 54048)
SR #1325 (1986), NR #92001812 (1993),
☒ 1719

Pendleton Ruin (LA 1369)
SR #1307 (1986), NR #92001794 (1993),
☒ 1719

Pigpen Creek Site (LA 54031)
SR #1318 (1986), NR #92001806 (1993),
☒ 1719

Saddle Bronc Site (Battleground Site) (LA 54039)
SR #1323 (1986), NR #92001810 (1993),
☒ 1719

Stewart Ranch Site (LA 54026)
SR #1315 (1986), NR #92001803 (1993),
☒ 1719

Sycamore Well Site (LA 5698)
SR #1310 (1986), NR #92001797 (1993),
☒ 1719

Timberlake Ruin (LA 54038)
SR #1322 (1986), NR #92001809 (1993),
☒ 1719

Anthony *(Doña Ana County)*

Gadsden High School (Valley High School)
NM 28
SR #1546 (1992)

Apache Creek *(Catron County)*

Apache Creek Ruin (LA 2949)
SR #92 (1969)

Aragon *(Catron County)*

Tularosa Cave (LA 4427)
NM 12
SR #125 (1969)

Arrey *(Sierra County)*

LA 50751
SR #1195 (1985), ☒ 1711

LA 517
SR #1207 (1985), NR #88000473 (1989), ☒ 1711

Percha Diversion Dam
SR #570 (1978), NR #79001555 (1979)

Bingham *(Socorro County)*

LA 1070
SR #1552 (1993), NR #93000244 (1993), ☒ 1550

LA 1071
SR #1553 (1993), NR #93000245 (1993), ☒ 1550

LA 1072
SR #1554 (1993), NR #93000246 (1993), ☒ 1550

LA 1074
SR #1556 (1993), NR #93000248 (1993), ☒ 1550

LA 1075
SR #1557 (1993), NR #93000249 (1993), ☒ 1550

LA 1076
SR #1558 (1993), NR #93000250 (1993), ☒ 1550

LA 1181
SR #1559 (1993), NR #93000251 (1993), ☒ 1550

LA 1201
SR #1560 (1993), NR #93000252 (1993), ☒ 1550

Launch Complex 33 (White Sands Missile Range V-2 Launch Site) ▲ (in Doña Ana County)
Nike Ave., White Sands Missile Range
SR #580 (1978), NR #85003541 (1985)

The German V-2 (*Vergeltungswaffen-2,* or "weapon of retaliation") rocket, created by the Nazis, was the most advanced rocket of World War II. At the end of the war, the American government captured hundreds of V-2s, as well as numerous German scientists and engineers associated with their development, including Dr. Werner Von Braun. In 1946, the Army brought Von Braun and the captured V-2s to the newly opened White Sands Missile Range to create and launch an American V-2. The White Sands V-2 Launch Site, also known as Launch Complex 33, was developed specifically to test V-2s; it represents the first generation of rocket testing that eventually led to the American exploration of space. The site consists of an Army blockhouse and a launching crane, known as the "gantry crane." The blockhouse, completed in 1945, was used mainly as a close-range observation point and laboratory. The blockhouse is 2400 square feet, with 10-foot thick walls and a 27-foot thick pyramidal roof of solid reinforced concrete. The gantry crane, completed in 1946, is a steel tower 75 feet tall and 25 feet wide with four platform levels for the placement of various types of rockets. The crane was modified for other tests after the completion of the V-2 program, but has now been restored to its original V-2 configuration.

Mockingbird Gap Archaeological Site (LA 26748)

SR #161 (1970)

Pueblo Oso Negro (LA 1073)

SR #1555 (1993), NR #93000247 (1993), ⊠ 1550

Pueblo Tinto (LA 1069)

SR #1551 (1993), NR #93000243 (1993), ⊠ 1550

Trinity Site ▲

US 380 on White Sands Missile Range

SR #30 (1968), NR #66000493 (1966)

Trinity Site on the White Sands Missile Range is in the basin formed by the San Andres Mountains to the west and the Sierra Oscura to the east. Ranches occupied this area before 1900, including the McDonald Ranch which was probably built around 1910 and was evacuated when the U.S. government established the Alamogordo Bombing Range in 1942. In 1944 this ranch was selected, because of its isolation, as the base camp for the Trinity Project, the test of the world's first nuclear fission bomb, developed 200 miles away in Los Alamos. The code name for the test was chosen by Project director, J. Robert Oppenheimer. The Trinity Site included concrete control and instrumentation bunkers with observation apertures and unmanned instrumentation bunkers with equipment to record the blast. On July 13, the final components of the bomb were delivered to the assembly site at the deserted McDonald Ranch two miles southeast of Ground Zero, the blast site. The world's first nuclear device was exploded on July 16, 1945. The 100-foot tower on which the bomb was detonated was vaporized by the blast, but Ground Zero, now marked by an obelisk of lava rock, still contains the remains of four concrete piers that supported the bomb tower. It is at the center of a 1600-foot diameter depression, caused by the blast, which was once covered with trinitite, a low-grade greenish glass fused from the soil by the heat of the bomb. The site is open to visitors biannually.

Caballo *(Sierra County)*

Small House North of Arroyo Seco (Yeo) (LA 1119)

SR #1206 (1985), NR #88000489 (1989), ⊠ 1711

Chamizal *(Socorro County)*

Sarracino Hall

Polvadera

SR #885 (1982)

Chloride *(Sierra County)*

Austin Crawford House

Wall St.

SR #1689 (1997)

Monte Christo Saloon
Wall St.
SR #1539 (1991)

Old Stone House
Wall St.
SR #1688 (1997)

Pioneer Store
Wall St.
SR #1538 (1991)

Claunch *(Socorro County)*

Gran Quivira National Monument and Collections (Salinas National Monument)
NM 10
SR #64 (1969), NR #66000494 (1966)

Seco Ruin (LA 9029)
SR #1590 (1994), NR #94000614 (1994) , ☒ 1550

Cliff *(Grant County)*

Kwilleyleka Ruin (LA 4937)
SR #221 (1971)

Woodrow Ruin (LA 2454)
SR #126 (1969), NR #70000402 (1970)

Columbus *(Luna County)*

Village of Columbus and Camp Furlong ▲
Portions of Columbus and Pancho Villa State Park
SR #390 (1975), SR #315 (1975), NR #75001164 (1975)

Most of the historic buildings of Columbus were built along the El Paso and Southwestern Railroad around 1902. Though railroad operations ceased in 1959 and the rails were removed in 1964, the track bed remains as a visual link between the buildings and as a reminder of the past. Near the depot was Camp Furlong, a United States military installation garrisoned by the 13th U.S. Cavalry, assigned to guard the international border from Noria to Hermanas. Early on March 9, 1916, Villista soldiers crossed from Mexico into Columbus and killed sixteen or more American soldiers and civilians; they were led by Francisco (Pancho) Villa. The famous bandit turned revolutionary had briefly controlled the Mexican government in 1914, occupying Mexico City while his rival, Venustiano Carranza, withdrew. In 1915, however, President Woodrow Wilson recognized Carranza's government, and Villa returned to guerilla warfare and attacks on Americans. He may have raided Columbus in the hope of restoring his failing fortunes by making himself indispensable in the defense of Mexico against foreign invasion. In response to the raid, Wilson sent a 6,000-man expeditionary force under General John J. Pershing, which ventured 300 miles into Mexico but never found Villa; they withdrew after an inconclusive 11 months. The supply center of the expedition was Camp Furlong, and the Columbus airfield was used as the base of the 1st Aero Squadron that supported Pershing's incursion into Mexico; it was the first operational military airbase in the United States. Pancho Villa's raid on Columbus was the last occasion on which foreign troops invaded the United States. Historic buildings that remain include the 1902 railroad depot, which is now a museum, and the pumphouse, customs house and section house; the Richard Rodriguez House; the Hoover Hotel; Camp Furlong's Recreation Hall and two adobe structures that served as officers' quarters; a brick schoolhouse; and the airfield. The museum in the depot and Camp Furlong are open to visitors.

Railroad Station Complex, Columbus
SR #319 (1974), VILLAGE OF COLUMBUS AND CAMP FURLONG DISTRICT

Cuchillo *(Sierra County)*

LA 50548
SR #1208 (1985), NR #88000488 (1989), ☒ 1711

Datil *(Catron County)*

Ake Site (LA 13423)
SR #424 (1975), NR #76001193 (1976)

Deming *(Luna County)*

Cook's Spring
SR #548 (1977)

Deming Armory
301 S. Silver Ave.
SR #584 (1978), NR #83001624 (1983)

The Deming Armory, completed in 1915, was built in response the revolution sweeping Mexico and fears of invasion or guerrilla attacks across the border, which did indeed happen at Columbus, New Mexico. It was also a response to the war in Europe, later to become World War I, and the possibility that the United States might be drawn into the conflict. The two-story brick building on a poured concrete foundation was designed by prominent architects Trost and Trost of El Paso, responsible for many of New Mexico's public buildings. The main entry is an arch and lobby leading to a double metal door. The facade has a decorative concrete parapet and coats of arms to suggest the military function of the building. The armory has a pitched roof above an attic that can be reached by hinged retractable steps, as well as a full basement, which was designed as a social and meeting area for Guard members, with chairs, reading tables, card rooms, locker rooms and showers. The long room on the north side of the basement was equipped for target practice, and was also a bowling alley and billiard room. The main floor was a drill hall with a maple floor. The armory, in use by the National Guard until 1976, illustrates America's transition from national to international military and political stature.

Deming Main Post Office
201 W. Spruce St.
SR #42, NR #90000139 (1990), ⊠ 1704

Seaman Field House (U.S. Customs House)
304 S. Silver Ave.
SR #1499 (1989), NR #90000102 (1990)

Fort Cummings (LA 8777)
SR #35 (1968)

100 S. Gold Avenue
SR #1388 (1987), ⊠ 1772

110 S. Gold Avenue
SR #1389 (1987), ⊠ 1772

200 S. Gold Avenue
SR #1390 (1987), ⊠ 1772

202 S. Gold Avenue
SR #1391 (1987), ⊠ 1772

Luna County Courthouse and Courthouse Park
700 S. Silver Ave.
SR #292 (1973), NR #77000925 (1977), ⊠ 1722

Mahoney Building
Gold St. and Spruce St.
SR #769 (1980), NR #80002551 (1980)

112-120 E. Spruce Street
SR #1394 (1987), ⊠ 1772

113 E. Spruce Street
SR #1393 (1987), ⊠ 1772

118 E. Pine Street
SR #1392 (1987), ⊠ 1772

105-107 N. Silver Avenue
SR #1385 (1987), ⊠ 1772

114 N. Silver Avenue
SR #1387 (1987), ⊠ 1772

116 N. Silver Avenue
SR #1386 (1987), ⊠ 1772

Silver Avenue Historic District
Silver Ave. between Pine St. and Spruce St.
SR #1384 (1987), ⊠ 1772

Derry *(Sierra County)*

Garfield Site (LA 1082)
SR #1193 (1985), ⊠ 1711

LA 50743
SR #1194 (1985), ⊠ 1711

LA 50749
SR #1196 (1985), ⊠ 1711

Doña Ana *(Doña Ana County)*

Doña Ana Village Historic District
North and south of NM 320 and west of I-25 interchange
SR #1641 (1996), NR #96001042 (1996)

Our Lady of Purification Catholic Church
Camino Real and 2nd St.
SR #927 (1983), NR #85001386 (1985)

Rio Grande Bridge - El Paso & Southwestern Railway
SR #725 (1979)

Dwyer *(Grant County)*

Trinidad Andazola House
NM 61, south of Eby Ranch Rd.
SR #1435 (1988), NR #88000500 (1988), ⊠ 1714

Ramon Baca House
NM 61, north of Grant-Luna County Line
SR #1436 (1988), NR #88000501 (1988),
☒ 1714

Tom Eby Storage Building
NM 61, north of Eby Ranch Rd.
SR #1432 (1988), NR #88000514 (1988),
☒ 1714

Montoya Site (LA 15075)
SR #502 (1977)

NAN Ranch
NM 61
SR #1431 (1988), NR #88000509 (1988),
☒ 1714

Soliz/Baca House
NM 61, south of Eby Ranch Rd.
SR #1434 (1988), NR #88000518 (1988),
☒ 1714

Maria J. and Juan Trujillo House
NM 61, south of Eby Ranch Rd.
SR #1433 (1988), NR #88000516 (1988),
☒ 1714

Upton Site (Pruitt Ruin) (LA 15030)
SR #504 (1977), NR #80002552 (1980)

Elephant Butte *(Sierra County)*

Elephant Butte Dam
Off NM 51
SR #617 (1978), NR #79001556 (1979),
ELEPHANT BUTTE HISTORIC DISTRICT

Named for Elephant Butte, a nearby geological formation, Elephant Butte Reservoir, with a capacity of over two million acre feet, was completed in 1916 to hold the periodic torrential floods of the Rio Grande and to provide a dependable water supply for irrigation. The dam, rising two hundred feet above the bed of the Rio Grande, with a crest length of twelve hun-

dred feet, contains 600,000 cubic yards of concrete, making it one of the largest engineering structures built up to that time. It has a four hundred foot spillway at the west end and four large wells for additional spillway capacity. Twelve outlets with steel gates draw water from the reservoir, driving turbine wheels for the hydroelectric plant. Private efforts to build a dam here began in the 1890s, but were thwarted when the Mexican government voiced fears that such as dam would interfere with navigation along the Rio Grande. Although the U.S. Circuit Court dismissed the complaint on the grounds that the Rio Grande was not navigable, the U.S. Justice Department found that the proposed project violated Mexico's rights to Rio Grande water. The U.S. Reclamation Service pushed for the dam, setting off a historic debate about interstate and international aspects of water use. After a 1906 treaty with Mexico made the dam possible, Congress appropriated funds for construction. A rail line to haul machinery, supplies and materials twelve miles from Engle was completed in 1911. Construction of the dam and reservoir took nearly seven years and cost more than five million dollars. Completed in May, 1916, Elephant Butte was then the largest manmade reservoir in the world.

Elephant Butte Historic District
From Ash Canyon to Mescal Canyon and north to long ridge
SR #1642 (1996), NR #96001616 (1997)

Escondida *(Socorro County)*

La Parida (LA 31718)
SR #1233 (1986)

Fairacres *(Doña Ana County)*

Picacho Lodge (Picacho School)
Bamert Dr. and US 70-80
SR #1375 (1987)

Gila *(Grant County)*

L. C. Ranch Headquarters
Off US 260
SR #189 (1970), NR #78001816 (1978)

Gila Cliff Dwelling National Monument *(Catron County)*

Black Mountain Lookout Cabin
On Black Mountain
SR #1442 (1988), NR #87002474 (1988), ☒ 1708

Gila Cliff Dwellings National Monument
SR #63 (1969), NR #66000472 (1966)

Gila Cliff Dwellings National Monument, comprising 533 acres, was established in 1907. Thirty-three recorded archaeological sites within the Monument span the development of the Mimbres Branch of the Mogollon culture from the late Archaic period (about 300 B.C.) through early and late pithouse periods to Classic and Post-Classic occupations (ending about A.D. 1300). The cliff dwellings, which date from the late 1270s through the early 1300s, consist of 42 rooms built of Gila Conglomerate quarried on the site, in a series of five natural south-facing caves. Ten to fifteen families probably occupied the cliff dwellings at any given time. Although the cliff dwellings and some other sites were vandalized before federal acquisition, most sites within the Monument were undisturbed. This is unique in the Mimbres area, where most Classic sites have been looted for their distinctive white ceramics with black designs, which people have come to associate with New Mexico. Many of these sites have been totally destroyed. A self-guided walking tour leads to the cliff dwellings.

Collections at the Gila Visitor Center
NM 15
SR #214 (1971)

Hachita *(Grant County)*

Old Hatchet Mine (LA 50085)
SR #721 (1979)

Hatch *(Doña Ana County)*

Pelham House
US 85
SR #1373 (1987)

St. Francis de Sales Church (Old Rodey Church)
Town Plaza, Rodey
SR #1255 (1986)

Hillsboro *(Sierra County)*

Alert/Hatcher Building
Second Ave. and Main St.
SR #1601 (1994), NR #95000460 (1995), HILLSBORO HISTORIC DISTRICT, ☒ 1600

William H. Bucher House
300 W. Main St.
SR #1603 (1994), NR #95000461 (1995), HILLSBORO HISTORIC DISTRICT, ☒ 1600

Hillsboro High School (Sierra County High School)
Elenora St.
SR #1549 (1993), NR #93000254 (1993)

Sierra County High School, which later became Hillsboro High School, was built in the summer of 1922 according to plans prepared by the El Paso architecture firm of Trost and Trost, the leading firm in the wide area of West Texas, Arizona and New Mexico for three decades. Though Sierra County was one of the major metal-producing counties in the state, population growth was slow. Hillsboro began as a mining camp and, when Sierra County was organized in 1884, it became the county seat. The high school was the first secondary school available to all students living in the county and the first structure built solely as a four-year high school. The building is a flat-roofed adobe covered with cement stucco in Mission Style, a style brought to New Mexico in the early part of the 20th century from California by the railroad. The plan, refined by Trost and Trost, is similar to the basic four-room adobe schoolhouse design produced by the Nebraska firm of Johnston Brothers, under commission by the Territorial Superintendent of Public Instruction. It contains four classrooms, a principal's office and a large

auditorium, arranged symmetrically around a patio.

Hillsboro Historic District
NM 90
SR #1304 (1986)

Meyers House
Main St. between 4th Ave. and 5th Ave.
SR #1605 (1994), NR #95000463 (1995), HILLSBORO HISTORIC DISTRICT, ☒ 1600

George Tambling and Ninette Stocker Miller House
South side of Elenora St., west of Union Church
SR #385 (1975), NR #95000465 (1995), ☒ 1600

Tom Murphy House
Elenora St.
SR #386 (1975), HILLSBORO HISTORIC DISTRICT

Percha Creek Bridge
NM 152 over Percha Creek
SR #1667 (1997), NR #97000731 (1997), ☒ 1661

Will M. Robins House
Main St. and 5th Ave.
SR #1604 (1994), NR #95000462 (1995), HILLSBORO HISTORIC DISTRICT, ☒ 1600

Cornelius (Neil) Sullivan House
Elenora and 1st Ave.
SR #1602 (1994), NR #95000459 (1995), HILLSBORO HISTORIC DISTRICT, ☒ 1600

Union Community Church
SR #389 (1975)

John M. Webster House (Robinson House)
Main St. and 5th Ave.
SR #1606 (1994), NR #95000464 (1995), HILLSBORO HISTORIC DISTRICT, ⊠ 1600

Kingston *(Sierra County)*

Hillsboro Peak Lookout Tower and Cabin
Gila National Forest
SR #1443 (1988), NR #87002475 (1988), ⊠ 1708

Percha Bank
Main St.
SR #179 (1970)

La Mesa *(Doña Ana County)*

San Jose Catholic Church
317 E. Josephine St.
SR #1283 (1986), NR #92001817 (1993)

La Mesilla *(Doña Ana County)*

Mesilla Historic District
Vicinity of Mesilla Plaza
SR #776 (1980), NR #82003323 (1982)

Mesilla Plaza ▲
2 miles south of Las Cruces on NM 28
SR #14 (1968), NR #66000475 (1966)

Mesilla was founded in 1849 in what was then a part of Mexico. The town began as a cluster of *jacal* (pole) structures around a central plaza, for defense against Indian raids. After the Gadsden Purchase of 1853, when Mesilla became part of the United States, the *jacales* were replaced with Territorial style adobe buildings. These were usually one story, with flat roofs, parapets capped with a coping of brick or masonry and thick 2- to 3-foot walls. They were built close to the property line, many with a small interior courtyard. Windows and doors were usually flush with the outside wall and built of milled lumber. Before 1881, when the railroad bypassed the town in favor of nearby Las Cruces, Mesilla was a prosperous town and the county seat of Doña Ana County. The plaza and remaining historic structures, including structures which were once stores, houses, the county courthouse, and the Butterfield Overland Stage and Mail Depot, date between 1849 and 1885. The Church of San Albino was built in 1906 to replace an 1857 adobe church.

Barela/Reynolds House
Mesilla Plaza
SR #248 (1972), NR #78001815 (1978), MESILLA HISTORIC DISTRICT

Former Dona Ana County Courthouse in Mesilla
Calle de Parian
SR #1261 (1986), MESILLA PLAZA DISTRICT, ⊠ 1722

Las Cruces *(Doña Ana County)*

Air Science Building (NMSU)
N. Horseshoe and Espina St.
SR #1456 (1988), NR #88001546 (1989), ⊠ 1707

Alameda/Depot Historic District
Around Pioneer Park and Alameda Blvd.
SR #773 (1980), NR #85000786 (1985)

The earliest residential suburbs were added to the original 1849 Las Cruces townsite after the arrival of the Atchison, Topeka and Santa Fe Railroad in 1881. The Alameda / Depot Historic District, which consists of 42 blocks and 192 historically or architecturally significant structures, is in an area about half a mile wide between the original townsite of Las Cruces and the railroad tracks; the district centers on a park near the railroad depot and extends up Alameda Boulevard, which represents a portion of the old Camino Real or Chihuahua Trail used since the 1500s. The architecture of the homes in the district combines vernacular adobe types and styles such as Territorial and Pueblo Revival with other regional American styles brought by the railroad, including Gothic, Queen Anne, Georgian and Colonial Revival, Italianate, Neo-Classical Revival, Prairie, Western Stick, Shingle, Mission Revival, and Bungalow. Some styles appeared in fanciful combinations in the same buildings. This mainly residential area demonstrates the historic importance of transportation routes to settlement and to architectural development in New Mexico.

Amador Building
Amador Ave. and Water St.
SR #44 (1969)

Nestor Armijo House
Lohman Ave. and Church St.
SR #54 (1969), NR #76001195 (1976)

Cade Property
169 W. Greening Ave.
SR #1630 (1996)

Court Junior High School
SR #1500 (1989), ALAMEDA/DEPOT HISTORIC DISTRICT

Former Doña Ana County Courthouse in Las Cruces
251 W. Amador
SR #1276 (1986), ⊠ 1722

Doña Ana County Courts Building (Old Post Office)
Church St. and Griggs Ave.
SR #1266 (1986), ⊠ 1722

Elephant Butte Irrigation District (Rio Grande Project)
Between Caballo Dam and El Paso, Texas
SR #1658 (1997), NR #97000822 (1997)

Fort Filmore
SR #36 (1969), NR #74001196 (1974)

Foster Hall (NMSU)
S. Horseshoe and Sweet
SR #1457 (1988), NR #88001547 (1989), ⊠ 1707

Goddard Hall (NMSU)
S. Horseshoe between Espina and Sweet
SR #1458 (1988), NR #88001548 (1988), ⊠ 1707

In 1889, Hiram Hadley established Las Cruces College, which was transformed into the New Mexico College of Agriculture and Mechanic Arts, a name it retained until 1960 when it became New Mexico State University. Goddard Hall is one of the original campus buildings built on the "horseshoe," the campus core, as part of a 1906 campus plan prepared by prominent El Paso architects Trost and Trost. The building was designed by O.H. Thorman using traditional Mission Style to continue the stylistic precedent of the Trost plan, (though only one other building followed this precedent). Goddard Hall is a three-story, masonry and stucco building with a hipped, French tile roof with a wide overhang and exposed rafters, arched windows and a bell tower over the entrance. There is a large 1936 addition on the east side of the building, but most of Goddard Hall is in original condition. The building has provided classroom space since it opened in 1913.

Albino Guerra House
Union Ave. and Laguna
SR #1370 (1987)

Hadley/Ludwick House (Hiram Hadley House)
2640 El Paseo Rd.
SR #1535 (1991), NR #91000352 (1991)

167 West Luceros
SR #832 (1981), ALAMEDA/DEPOT HISTORIC DISTRICT

Mason Ranche Site (Slocums' Ranche) (LA 26993)
SR #1562 (1993)

Mesquite Street Original Townsite Historic District
Bounded by E. Texas, Campo, Tornillo and E. Court
SR #777(1980), NR #85001669 (1985)

Rhodes/Garrett/Hamiel Dormitory (NMSU)
SR #446 (1976)

University President's House (NMSU)
University Ave. between Espina and Solano
SR #1459 (1988), NR #88001549 (1989), ⊠ 1707

Lemitar *(Socorro County)*

Sagrada Familia de Lemitar Church
SR #873 (1982), NR #83001631 (1983)

Lordsburg *(Hidalgo County)*

Shakespeare Ghost Town
Off NM 494
SR #41 (1969), NR #73001141 (1973)

Shakespeare was a stage stop on the legendary Butterfield Overland Mail Route to California. Several period structures remain at the site, which serves today as a ranch headquarters. It is open periodically for visitors and Old West events.

Hidalgo County Courthouse
300 S. Shakespeare St.
SR #1269 (1986), NR #87000897 (1987), ⊠ 1722

Hidalgo Hotel
328 E. Motel Dr.
SR #1541 (1992)

Lordsburg Coaling Tower
SR #719 (1979)

The Lordsburg Coaling Tower, located on the north side of the railroad tracks near what was once the Southern Pacific Depot, is a reinforced concrete structure thirty feet square and ninety feet high, with a fifteen-foot square elevator shaft on the northwest corner. When the tower was built for the

Southern Pacific Company in 1926, during the years of coal-fired steam locomotives, coaling towers were common. The lower part of the tower was open to allow trains to pass through, delivering coal to the elevator. Two hoppers received stored coal (the tower had a capacity of 200 tons) and passed it by means of movable metal chutes to locomotive tenders on the adjacent tracks. The introduction of oil-fired steam locomotives and diesels made the coaling tower obsolete, and the Lordsburg tower was taken out of service in 1951. Most of the machinery and metal parts were removed, but the tower still looks much as it did when it was built; it is one of the few remaining railroad coaling facilities in New Mexico.

Shakespeare Cemetery
Banner Mine Rd. and 85 Mine Rd.
SR #40 (1969), SHAKESPEARE GHOST TOWN

Stein's Peak Station
SR #198 (1970)

Magdalena *(Socorro County)*

Alamo School Pueblo Site (LA 19208)
SR #778 (1980)

Aragon House
2nd St. and Oak St.
SR #865 (1982), NR #82003327(1982), ☒ 1698

Atchison, Topeka & Santa Fe Railway Depot
Off US 60
SR #410 (1975), NR #78001829 (1978), ☒ 1698

Bank of Magdalena
1st St. and Main St.
SR #412 (1975), NR #82003328 (1982), ☒ 1698

Clemens Ranch House
SR #378 (1975), NR #79001557 (1979)

Dobson House
SR #866 (1982), ☒ 1698

Gallinas Springs Ruin (LA 1178)
SR #101 (1969), NR #70000413 (1970)

Gutierrez House
3rd St. and Poplar St.
SR #870 (1982), NR #82003329 (1982), ☒ 1698

Hall Hotel
2nd St. and Spruce St.
SR #867 (1982), NR #82003330 (1982), ☒ 1698

Hilton House
US 60
SR #872 (1982), NR #82003331 (1982), ☒ 1698

Charles Ilfeld Company Warehouse
Main St.
SR #441 (1976), NR #82003332 (1982), ☒ 1698

Kelly Mine (Magdalena Mining District)
Off US 60, Kelly
SR #556 (1978)

In the 19th century, Kelly Mine, the center of the Magdalena Mining District, produced both lead and silver. Kelly became a significant mining area around 1885 shortly after a branch line of the Atchison, Topeka and Santa Fe Railroad was extended from Socorro to Magdalena; a daily stage ran between Magdalena and Kelly. The lead and silver were eventually depleted, but the mine became important again in 1902 when smithsonite, a valuable zinc carbonate, was discovered by Cory T.Brown of Socorro, who tested the greenish rock that he noticed in the mine's waste piles. At the turn of the century, Kelly's Graphic

Mine, owned by Brown and his partner, J.B. Fitch, led the state in zinc production. Smithsonite deposits were exhausted by the early 1930s, and Kelly declined and was eventually abandoned. All that remain of the extensive mining operations are mine tailings, adobe and rock ruins, abandoned buildings and head frames. Only the Catholic church is still in fair condition.

Lewellen House
2nd St. and Chestnut St.
SR #868 (1982), NR #82003333 (1982),
⊠ 1698

Little Mission Church of St. John the Baptist
Kelly
SR #376 (1975)

MacTavish House
Elm St.
SR #871 (1982), NR #82003334 (1982),
⊠ 1698

Magdalena Historic District
SR #312 (1974)

Magdaline House
3rd St. and Chestnut St.
SR #869 (1982), NR #82003335 (1982),
⊠ 1698

Main Street Commercial Building
Main St.
SR #862 (1982), NR #82003336 (1982),
⊠ 1698

Salome Store
1st St.
SR #863 (1982), NR #82003337 (1982),
⊠ 1698

Salome Store Warehouse
1st St.
SR #864 (1982), NR #82003338 (1982),
⊠ 1698

Mimbres *(Grant County)*

Hooks/Moore Store
NM 61 and FR 73
SR #1418 (1988), NR #88000490 (1988),
⊠ 1714

Otto Huechling House
East of NM 61
SR #1421 (1988), NR #88000496 (1988),
⊠ 1714

Janss Site (LA 12077)
SR #500 (1977), NR #80002550 (1980)

Mattocks Site (LA 676)
SR #501 (1977), NR #80002548 (1980)

Mimbres School
East of NM 61 and FR 73
SR #1419 (1988), NR #88000491 (1988),
⊠ 1714

William Redding House
East of NM 61
SR #1417 (1988), NR #88000483 (1988),
⊠ 1714

Reeds Peak Lookout Tower
On Reeds Peak
SR #1440 (1988), NR #87002472 (1988),
⊠ 1708

George Sibole Store
NM 61, north of FR 73
SR #1416 (1988), NR #88000482 (1988),
⊠ 1714

Ysabel Valencia House
East of NM 61
SR #1420 (1988), NR #88000493 (1988),
⊠ 1714

Dr. Granville Wood House
East of NM 61
SR #1422 (1988), NR #88000498 (1988),
⊠ 1714

Mogollon *(Catron County)*

Nick Ayon Saloon
SR #301 (1973)

Bearwallow Mountain Lookout Cabins and Shed
Bearwallow Mountain
SR #1441 (1988), NR #87002473 (1988),
⊠ 1708

Coate's and Howard General Store
Lot 21, Imperial Addition
SR #536 (1977)

Fannie Hill Mill and Company Town Historic District
SR #1413 (1988), NR #87001567 (1987)

Gold and silver were first discovered in the Mogollon region in 1870 by James Cooney, a U.S. Cavalry scout stationed at Fort Bayard eighty miles to the south. Frank

Vingo established the Little Fannie Mine in 1887 and in the same year built the first house in Mogollon. The mill was the largest producer of gold and silver in New Mexico from 1908 to 1925. It used the new cyanide process that, compared with the old mercury pan amalgamation process, revolutionized the milling of gold and silver. The remains of the mill and the town are a reminder of the important role of mining in New Mexico's economy in the early part of the century. It is also one of the best-preserved historic mining mills in the state. At the time the Fannie Hill company town was established, the company town was a new concept, part of the rationale that accommodating workers would boost productivity. The company town at Fannie Hill Mill was laid out and designed by mine engineers, and was well-constructed, though without frills, providing what was needed without reducing profits. The 29 remaining buildings from about 1908-1942 are wood frame with corrugated metal roofs; the only original ornaments were the Bungalow-style brackets on the porch of the manager's house. The town includes the manager's house, workers' houses, a hospital and a company store. These buildings line both sides of a single road that runs from the east end of the district to the main ridge of Fannie Hill at the middle of the district. A power plant stands on the crest of the ridge. The headframe and mill of the Fannie Hill Mine are located below an arm of the road, with a machine shop, assay office, general storehouse and blacksmith shop just above the road.

Johns Brothers House (Topsey Mine)
SR 78
SR #664 (1978), MOGOLLON HISTORIC DISTRICT (MOGOLLON GHOST TOWN)

Little Fannie Mine
SR 78
SR #563 (1978), MOGOLLON HISTORIC DISTRICT (MOGOLLON GHOST TOWN)

Mogollon Baldy Lookout Cabin
On Mogollon Baldy Peak
SR #1438 (1988), NR #87002470 (1988), ⊠ 1708

Mogollon Historic District (Mogollon Ghost Town)
SR 78 (Bursum Rd.)
SR #38 (1969), NR #87001541 (1987)

Mogollon Theater
SR 78
SR #475 (1976), MOGOLLON HISTORIC DISTRICT (MOGOLLON GHOST TOWN)

Mogollon Village Site (LA 11568)
SR #306 (1979)

Whitewater Canyon Pipeline
On Whitewater Creek
SR #581 (1977)

Nutt *(Sierra County)*

Lake Valley Mining District
Lake Valley
SR #559 (1978)

Lake Valley School House
Lake Valley
SR #431 (1976), LAKE VALLEY MINING DISTRICT

Old Horse Springs
(Catron County)

Bat Cave (LA 4935)
SR #93 (1969), NR #76001194 (1976)

Bat Cave, in the Mogollon Highlands, is a complex of adjacent rock shelters eroded from volcanic conglomerate by the waves of the lake that filled the San Augustin Plains in Pleistocene times. The shelters are about 128 feet above the current surface of the Plains. From 4000 B.C. to about A.D. 1100, the cave was used at various times as a habitation by prehistoric Indians. Bat Cave, like other sites in the Mogollon Highlands such as Tularosa Cave, Cordova Cave and Cienega Creek, is one of the earliest agricultural sites in the Southwest. Between about 1500 B.C. and 300 B.C., domestic plants including maize, squash, beans and bottle gourd reached New Mexico from the south. When Bat Cave was excavated in 1948 and 1950, in addition to projectile points and other stone and bone artifacts, evidence of these crops were found in the cave. The maize found in Bat Cave dates to 1350 B.C., one of the earliest dates for agriculture in

the Southwest. Bat Cave is not accessible to the public.

Mangas Mountain Lookout Complex
Mangas Mountain
SR #1439 (1988), NR #87002471 (1988), ☒ 1708

Pie Town *(Catron County)*

Tom's Rock Pueblo (LA 55366)
SR #1302 (1986), ☒ 1721

Pinos Altos *(Grant County)*

Pinos Altos Historic District
Bounded by Gold Ave., Cherry St., Main St., Church St., and Silver St.
SR #917 (1983), NR #84002945 (1984)

Gold Avenue Methodist Episcopal Church
Gold Ave.
SR #442 (1976), PINOS ALTOS HISTORIC DISTRICT

Quemado *(Catron County)*

El Caso Lookout Complex
Gila National Forest
SR #1444 (1988), NR #87002476 (1988), ☒ 1708

Hubble Corner Pueblo (LA 8112)
SR #1301 (1986), ☒ 1721

Radium Springs *(Doña Ana County)*

Fort Selden
SR # 47 (1969), NR #70000401 (1970)

Leasburg Dam
SR #562 (1978)

Rio Grande Bridge
NM 85
SR #574 (1978)

Rio Grande Bridge at Radium Springs
NM 185 over Rio Grande
SR #1663 (1997), NR #97000734 (1997), ☒ 1661

Red Hill *(Catron County)*

Cox Ranch Ruin (Mogollon Pueblo) (LA 13681)
SR #713 (1979), NR#78001811 (1978)

Goesling Ranch Pueblo (LA 3993)
SR #1299 (1986), ☒ 1721

Salt Lake *(Catron County)*

Zuni Salt Lake
SR #204 (1970)

San Antonio *(Socorro County)*

Fort Craig
SR #46 (1969), NR #70000414 (1970)

Fort Craig, established in 1854 to protect the Rio Abajo region from Navajo and Apache raids and to safeguard travelers between Santa Fe and El Paso, became significant during the Civil War. In 1861, nearby Fort Fillmore surrendered to the Confederate forces, and Fort Craig was

strengthened. Contingents from the post tried unsuccessfully to dislodge the Confederates from the area around Mesilla. When the Confederates began to move up the Rio Grande, troops from Fort Craig blocked their route at Valverde, just north of the fort, resulting in the first major battle of the Civil War in the Southwest in 1862. The Confederates captured the field, and as defeated Union troops withdrew to the fort, the Confederates pushed north capturing Albuquerque and Santa Fe, but were ultimately turned back by the loss of their supply train during the Battle of Glorieta Pass east of Santa Fe. During the 1860s, Fort Craig gave provisions and escorts to miners and travelers, but as Indian raids diminished, so did the fort's usefulness. The Army abandoned it in 1885, and materials from the fort were removed to build houses and other structures in the vicinity. The remains of Fort Craig include stone and adobe walls and mounds resulting from the collapse of the buildings, as well as the earthen embankment and ditch, built as fortifications at the outbreak of the Civil War. The site is now federal property. It has been stabilized and interpreted by the Bureau of Land Management and is open to the public.

Hilton Bar at the Owl Bar
SR #404 (1975)

Miera/Baca House
Main St. and 5th St.
SR #952 (1983)

Eutimio Montoya House
SR #614 (1978)

New Mexico State Bank Building
101 6th St.
SR #1005 (1984)

Paraje de Fra Cristobal (LA 1124)
SR #1231 (1986)

San Antonio de Acuinas Mission (LA 31745)
SR #1232 (1986)

Sandal Cave (LA 8696)
SR #116 (1969)

San Juan *(Grant County)*

George O. Perrault Compound
East of NM 61 and north of Mimbres Hot Springs Canyon Rd., Sherman
SR #1429 (1988), NR #88000507 (1988), ⊠ 1714

San Juan Historic District
2261-2291 NM 61
SR #1415 (1988), NR #88000481 (1988), ⊠ 1714

San Juan Teacherage
North of Mimbres Hot Springs Canyon Rd., Sherman
SR #1430 (1988), NR #88000508 (1988), ⊠ 1714

Jesus Valencia House
East of NM 61
SR #1428 (1988), NR #88000506 (1988), ⊠ 1714

Wheaton/Smith Site (LA 18903)
SR #505 (1977), NR #80002549 (1980)

San Lorenzo *(Grant County)*

San Lorenzo Historic District
West side of Galaz St. between G St. and D St.
SR #1414 (1988), NR #88000480 (1988), ⊠ 1714

Acklin Store
NM 90, west of junction with NM 61
SR #1425 (1988), NR #88000502 (1988), ⊠ 1714

Father Roger Aull House and Chapel
North end of Noonday Canyon Rd.
SR #1507 (1989)

Luciana B. Grijalva House
East of NM 61
SR #1423 (1988), NR #88C00499 (1988),
✖ 1714

Menard/Galaz House
West side of NM 90
SR #1424 (1988), NR #88C00503 (1988),
✖ 1714

Mauricio Portillo Homestead
East of NM 61
SR #1427 (1988), NR #88C00504 (1988),
✖ 1714

Antonio Torres House
NM 90
SR #1426 (1988), NR #88C00505 (1988),
✖ 1714

Santa Rita *(Grant County)*

Santa Rita Copper Mines Historic Site (LA 49996)
SR #619 (1978)

Copper was known and used by Pueblo people back to Classic times, around the 11th century A.D. When the Spanish arrived in Mexico, or what was then called New Spain, mining became the basis of Spain's imperial wealth and power. The mining frontier had been moving slowly northward for almost three centuries when a Spanish officer, Lt. Colonel José Manuel Carrasco, found the Santa Rita Copper Mine in 1800. He sold out to his financial backer, Don Francisco Elguea, who had the influence to obtain a concession of land and convict labor from the royal government. Elguea built a triangular adobe fort-prison on the site for convict laborers who dug deep shafts into the hills to the

ore, carrying it up long ladders in ore sacks hanging on their backs by a forehead strap. This early system was extremely primitive, and without stoppings and timbering, cave-ins buried many miners alive. Open pit mining methods pioneered in Utah were employed at Santa Rita in 1911. By the 1950s the community of Santa Rita had six thousand people, but the expanding pit eventually compelled the abandonment of the town. Today the vast pit, visible from an overlook, covers the area where Elguea held his fort against hostile Apaches.

Silver City *(Grant County)*

David Abraham House
603 Black St.
SR #185 (1970), SILVER CITY HISTORIC DISTRICT

H. B. Ailman House
312 W. Broadway
SR #186 (1970), NR #75001163 (1975), SILVER CITY HISTORIC DISTRICT

Bell Block
208-212 W. Broadway
SR #527 (11/20/77)

Black's Addition Historic District
Bounded by College, Black and Market
SR #882 (1982)

Bowden Hall (WNMU)
Northeast of Light Hall and southwest of Heating Plant
SR #1462 (1988), NR #88001552 (1988), WESTERN NEW MEXICO UNIVERSITY HISTORIC DISTRICT, ^1707

Minnie L. Brumback House
701 Bayard St.
SR #728 (1979)

Bullard Hotel
105 S. Bullard St.
SR #1408 (1988), NR #88000435 (1988)

The Bullard Hotel, which opened in Silver City in 1916, incorporated part of the 1883 Palace Hotel. A brick facade was added to the front of the Palace, but the rear of the older building remained the same, and it can still be seen that the brick is a different color. The hotel was part of a general modernization of the town that included street paving for the automobiles that were just coming into use, and the building was in an advantageous location two blocks south of Bullard and Broadway Streets, the main intersection of downtown Silver City, and one block north of the railroad depot. The new railroad depot, built in 1915, brought tourists and visitors, and the hotel was advertised as Silver City's most modern hotel, with steam heat and hot and cold running water in every room. The two-story brick building has a flat roof, double-hung windows and a symmetrical facade with a central recessed entrance with a balcony above it. The facade has projecting decorative courses of brick. The roof has low brick parapets that are capped with concrete for protection from the weather. The Bullard Hotel is the only hotel that remains from the period of Silver City's growth and prosperity that extended through World War I.

Chihuahua Hill Historic District
Bounded by Cooper, Spring, Bullard and Chihuahua
SR #906 (1982), NR #84002943 (1984)

Isaac N. Cohen House
511 N. Bullard St.
SR #850 (1982), SILVER CITY HISTORIC DISTRICT

Thomas Conway House
703 N. Texas St.
SR #528 (1977), SILVER CITY HISTORIC DISTRICT

Fleming Hall (WNMU)
10th St.
SR #1463 (1988), NR #88001553 (1988), WESTERN NEW MEXICO UNIVERSITY HISTORIC DISTRICT, ⊠ 1707

Graham Gymnasium (WNMU)
Florida St.
SR #1464 (1988), NR #88001554 (1988), WESTERN NEW MEXICO UNIVERSITY HISTORIC DISTRICT, ⊠ 1707

Grant County Courthouse
117 Cooper St.
SR #1271 (1986), SILVER CITY HISTORIC DISTRICT, ⊠ 1722

Bessie Harper House
905 W. 12th St.
SR #1596 (1994)

With the discovery of silver in the area in 1870, Silver City developed to serve the needs of the miners. In addition to more mundane services such as hotels, stores, schools, medical services, electricity and the railroad, prostitution was common, and Bessie Harper began her career as a madam in Silver City in the early 1880s. She was known as a smart businesswoman. In addition to building the houses at 901 and 905 W. 12th Street as rental properties, she had the financial sense to acquire other rentals

in respectable parts of town. The profession of landlady was acceptable for a single woman at the time, and the rentals also provided supplemental income. By 1914, Harper owned all the odd-numbered lots in Block 6 of Powel's Subdivision, where this house was built. Bessie Harper increased the number of her short-term rental properties about this time to serve the healthseekers who were coming to New Mexico. The Bessie Harper House is a classic one-story, red-brick bungalow on a concrete foundation. Its classic bungalow style and modest size were common in the United States at the time, but rare in Silver City. The house has been renovated with installation of a modern electrical system, plumbing system and kitchen.

Heating Plant (WNMU)
10th St.
SR #1465 (1988), NR #88001555 (1988), WESTERN NEW MEXICO UNIVERSITY HISTORIC DISTRICT, ⊠ 1707

Light Hall (WNMU)
College Ave. at B St.
SR #1466 (1988), NR #88001556 (1988), WESTERN NEW MEXICO UNIVERSITY HISTORIC DISTRICT, ⊠ 1707

C.W. Marriot House
615 W. 6th St.
SR #695 (1978)

Martin Maher House
Market St. and Pinos Altos St.
SR #190 (1970), SILVER CITY HISTORIC DISTRICT

Meredith and Ailman Bank Block
Bullard St. and Broadway
SR #533 (1977), SILVER CITY HISTORIC DISTRICT

Old Presbyterian Church
609 N. Arizona St.
SR #722 (1979), SILVER CITY HISTORIC DISTRICT

Ritch Hall (WNMU)
10th St.
SR #1467 (1988), NR #88001557 (1988), WESTERN NEW MEXICO UNIVERSITY HISTORIC DISTRICT, ⊠ 1707

Silver City Historic District
Bounded by Black, College, Hudson, and Spring St.
SR #197 (1970), NR #78001817 (1978)

Silver City North Addition Historic District
Bounded by the San Vicente Arroyo, College Ave., Chloride St. and 13th St.
SR #883 (1982), NR #83001620 (1983)

Silver City Water Works Building
Little Walnut Rd.
SR #916 (1983), NR #84002950 (1984)

In the late 19th century, Silver City was a well-established town with substantial amenities for a frontier community. In

addition to telegraph, railroad spur line and telephone service, the town installed its first electric light plant in 1884, only two years after a system was installed in New York City. In keeping with the quest for modernization, a water system was a priority in Silver City, both as a reliable means of water distribution in an arid environment and for fire protection. Silver City's early residents were concerned about fire prevention; the town purchased the first fire engine in the territory in 1875 and banned frame construction in 1880. The Silver City Water Works building, one of the few stone buildings in Silver City, was built in 1887 by George Utter, who was granted the franchise by the town council. A one-and-a-half story section with a cross gable roof was originally the engineer's residence. It is attached to a one-story, flat-roofed section with a raised stonework parapet, where the water works equipment was housed. In 1925, the water works were sold to the Town of Silver City; although the water works are no longer in the old stone building, they are still on the premises. Once located on open land on the far outskirts of the city, the building is now part of a residential neighborhood. The building is being refurbished using grants from the Historic Preservation Division and other funding.

Stine/Flemming House
603 Bayard St.
SR #193 (1970), SILVER CITY HISTORIC DISTRICT

St. Mary's Academy Historic District
1813 N. Alabama St.
SR #881 (1982), NR #83001621 (1983)

Treasure Hill Site (LA 16241)
Lone Mountain Rd.
SR #353 (1974)

O.S. Warren House
104 E. Market St.
SR #194 (1970), SILVER CITY HISTORIC DISTRICT

Western New Mexico University Historic District
SR #846 (1981)

Socorro *(Socorro County)*

212-214 E. Abeytia Ave.
SR #600 (1978), ☒ 656

216 E. Abeytia Ave.
SR #601 (1978), ☒ 656

Abeytia Block
101-105 Plaza
SR #506 (1977), SOCORRO MULTIPLE RESOURCE DISTRICT, ☒ 656

Aniceto Abeytia House
303 Eaton Ave.
SR #605 (1978), NR #91000032 (1991), SOCORRO MULTIPLE RESOURCE DISTRICT, ☒ 1534, ☒ 656

Alvarez/Briggs House
600 Nicholas Ave.
SR #621 (1978), SOCORRO MULTIPLE RESOURCE DISTRICT, ☒ 656

Atchison, Topeka & Santa Fe Railway Depot
706 Manzanares Ave. East
SR #620 (1978), ☒ 1534, ☒ 656

A.B. Baca House
201 School of Mines Rd.
SR #507 (1977), NR #91000036 (1991), ☒ 1534

Juan Jose Baca House
Abeyta St. and Plaza
SR #153 (1970), ☒ 656

Billing Smelter (Rio Grande Smelting Works)
Spring St.
SR #1540 (1991)

Bourguignon House
307 Mt. Carmel Rd.
SR #622 (1978)

Brown Hall (NMIMT)
NMIMT Campus
SR #1460 (1988), NR #88C01550 (1989), ☒ 1707

Brown House
205 Abeytia Ave. NE
SR #591 (1978), ^656

Bursum House
326 Church St.
SR #297 (1973), NR #75001172 (1975), ☒ 656

300 S. California St.
SR #602 (1978), ☒ 656

400 S. California St.
SR #603 (1978), ☒ 656

The Capitol
104 Plaza
SR #623 (1978), ☒ 656

509 Center
SR #604 (1978), ☒ 1534

Chambon House
324 Church Ave.
SR #298 (1973), ☒ 656

Chihuahua Historic District
Along Nicholas Ave., west of Pena Pl.
SR #651 (1978), ☒ 656

Church of the Epiphany
219 Fisher Ave.
SR #592 (1979), ☒ 656

Church/McCutcheon Historic District
Bounded by McCutcheon Ave., Church St., Eaton Ave. and Park St.
SR #652 (1978), ☒ 1534

Captain Michael Cooney House
309 McCutcheon Ave.
SR #624 (1978), NR #91000029 (1991), ☒ 1534, ☒ 656

Anthony Cortesy House
327 McCutcheon Ave.
SR #625 (1978), NR #91000033 (1991), ☒ 1534, ☒ 656

Crabtree Building
211 Fisher Ave.
SR #626 (1978), ☒ 656

Crown Mill
East of intersection of US 85 and railroad
SR #207 (1971), ☒ 656

East Abeytia Avenue Historic District
East Abeytia Ave.
SR #653 (1978), ☒ 656

Eaton House
403 Eaton Ave.
SR #308 (1974), ☒ 656

Nestor P. Eaton House (Eaton/Darr House)
313 McCutcheon Ave.
SR #627 (1978), NR #91000034 (1991), ☒ 656, ☒ 1534

El Torreon
305-317 Park St.
SR #628 (1978), ⊠ 656

217 Fisher Ave.
SR #640 (1978), ⊠ 656

249 Fisher Ave.
SR #606 (1978), ⊠ 656

Fitch Building
207 Fisher Ave.
SR #629 (1978), ⊠ 656

Fitch Hall (NMIMT)
SR #1461 (1988), NR #88001551 (1989), ⊠ 1707

James Gurden Fitch House
311 McCutcheon Ave.
SR #630 (1978), NR #91000035 (1991), ⊠ 1534, ⊠ 656

Fortune Property
110 Park St.
SR #593 (1978), ⊠ 656

Juan Nepomuceno Garcia Opera House
Terry Ave. and California St.
SR #158 (1970), NR #74001210 (1974), SAN MIGUEL HISTORIC DISTRICT

In the 1880s, Socorro was very prosperous as a result of silver mining and the arrival of the railroad. One of many public buildings constructed during this period was the Garcia Opera house, built in 1886 by Francisca Garcia, widow of Juan Nepomuceno Garcia and matriarch of a prominent local family. The Garcia Opera House is an example of the Greek Revival style which was popular in midwestern opera houses before it reached the west, but its adobe construction is typical of New Mexican architecture. The building has a pitched roof and an unusual open-trussed roof system to span the large interior space. The hardwood dance-floor and audience area was originally lined on both sides with a raised duena platform for chaperones. The stage took up one third of the floor space. The opera house was originally lighted with chandeliers and single wall lamps with reflectors. Francisca Garcia hoped that traveling opera companies would visit the house, and although this did not happen, the structure was used for fifty years by traveling theatrical troupes, as well as for masked balls, dances, school programs and even college basketball games. It functioned as a community center into the 1940s. After years of deterioration, the building was repaired and stabilized funded by a grant from the Historic Preservation Division.

Juan Nepomuceno Garcia House
108 Bernard St.
SR #157 (1970), NR #91000027 (1991), SAN MIGUEL HISTORIC DISTRICT, ⊠ 1534

304 Garfield St.
SR #641 (1978), ⊠ 656

Marcos Gonzales House
B St. and Texas Ave.
SR #922 (1983), ⊠ 1534

211 Grant Ave.
SR #607 (1978)

Herrick House
505 Center St.
SR #486 (1977), ⊠ 656

August Holver Hilton House
601 Park St.
SR #631 (1978), NR #91000031 (1991), ⊠ 1534, ⊠ 656

Illinois Brewery
Neal Ave. and 6th St.
SR #209 (1971), NR #75001173 (1975), ⊠ 1534

Keith House
405 Park St.
SR #647 (1978), NR #91000030 (1991), ⊠ 1534

Kittrel Park
Park, Plaza and Center St.
SR #923 (1983), ⊠ 1534, ⊠ 656

Kittrel Park/Manzanares Avenue Historic District
SR #654 (1983), ⊠ 656

Knights of Pythias Hall
106-106½ E. Manzanares Ave.
SR #594 (1978), ⊠ 656

Lowenstein/Torres House
403 NM 85
SR #632 (1978), ⊠ 656

101 E. Manzanares Ave.
SR #608 (1978), ⊠ 656

102 E. Manzanares Ave.
SR #609 (1978), ⊠ 656

108 E. Manzanares Ave.
SR #610 (1978), ⊠ 656

110 E. Manzanares Ave.
SR #611 (1978), ⊠ 656

315 McCutcheon Ave.
SR #642 (1978), ⊠ 656

605 Nicholas Ave.
SR #643 (1978), ⊠ 656

609 Nicholas Ave.
SR #644 (1978), ⊠ 656

613 Nicholas Ave.
SR #645 (1978), ⊠ 656

Park Hotel
Garfield St.
SR #595 (1978), ⊠ 656

301-303 Park St.
SR #646 (1978), ⊠ 656

Price/Loewenstein Mercantile
107 Manzanares Ave.
SR #596 (1978), ⊠ 656

San Felipe Pueblo Ruin (LA 597)
SR #793 (1980), NR #83001632 (1983)

San Miguel Historic District
SR #655 (1978), ⊠ 1534

201 San Miguel St.
SR #648 (1978), ⊠ 656

202 San Miguel St.
SR #613 (1978), ⊠ 1534

Church of San Miguel
Otero St.
SR #291 (1973), ⊠ 656

Anastacio Sedillo House
114 W. Baca St.
SR #590 (1978), SAN MIGUEL HISTORIC DISTRICT

Jacobo Sedillo House
348 Bernard St.
SR #633 (1978), ⊠ 656

110 N. Sixth St.
SR #612 (1978), ⊠ 656

201 Sixth St.
SR #649 (1978), ⊠ 656

Socorro County Courthouse
200 Church St.
SR #920 (1983), ⊠ 1534, ⊠ 1722

Socorro Plaza (Kittrel Park)
SR #351 (1974), ⊠ 1534

Edward S. Stapleton House
313 Mt. Carmel Rd.
SR #635 (1978), ☒ 656

Vivian Stapleton House
321 Mt. Carmel Rd.
SR #636 (1978), ☒ 656

Teypama Piro Site (LA 282)
SR #884 (1992), NR #83004179 (1983)

Torres Block
101-107 W. Manzanares Ave.
SR #597 (1978), ☒ 656

A.C. Torres House
408 US 85 S
SR #637 (1978), ☒ 656

Jesus Maria Torres House
225-225A Fisher Ave.
SR #921 (1978), ☒ 1534

Lupe Torres House
347 Bernard St.
SR #638 (1978), ☒ 656

Val Verde Hotel
203 Manzanares St.
SR #300 (1983), NR #77000930 (1977), ☒ 656

Rufina Vigil House (Casa de Flecha)
407 Park St.
SR #151 (1970), NR #91000028 (1991), ☒ 1534

White Row
300-306 Center St.
SR #598 (1978), ☒ 656

Delfine Zimmerly House
205 Mt. Carmel Rd.
SR #639 (1978), ☒ 656

Zingerle House
215 Bernard St.
SR #599 (1978)

Sunland Park *(Doña Ana County)*

American Diversion Dam
SR #714 (1979)

International Boundary Marker No. 1
SR #311 (1974), NR #74001195 (1974)

Truth or Consequences *(Sierra County)*

Alamosa Ranch House and Blacksmith Shop
Martin Ranch Rd.
SR #1023 (1984)

Caballo Dam
NM 85
SR #546 (1978)

Chambers Canyon Site (LA49028)
SR #1197 (1985), NR #88000485 (1989), ☒ 1711

Hedrick House
906 E. Riverside Dr.
SR #1493 (1989)

Horse Island Site (LA 48996)
SR #1199 (1985), NR #88000478 (1988), ☒ 1711

Hot Springs Main Post Office
400 Main St.
SR #242, NR #90000141 (1990), ☒ 1704

Kettle Top Butte Site (LA 48995)
SR #1200 (1985), NR #88000477 (1988), ☒ 1711

LA 49016
SR #1205 (1985), NR #88000484 (1989), ☒ 1711

LA 49030
SR #1202 (1985), NR #88000486 (1989), ☒ 1711

Las Palomas (LA 8707)

SR #1204 (1985), ⊠ 1711

Longbottom Canyon Ruin (LA 49033)

SR #1203 (1985), NR #88000487(1989), ⊠ 1711

Monticello Point Ruin and Archaelogical District (LA 48990-48994)

SR #1198 (1985), NR #88000476 (1988), ⊠ 1711

Palomas Narrows Ruin (LA 38755, LA 49007)

SR #1201 (1985), NR #88000475 (1989), NR #88000479 (1989), ⊠ 1711

Sierra Grande Lodge and Spa

501 McAdoo St.

SR #1691 (1997)

The town of Truth or Consequences, locally called "T or C," was renamed for a popular game show in 1950, but it was originally called Hot Springs for the natural mineral springs in the area. It developed as a result of the construction of the Elephant Butte Dam, with stores selling goods to the workers. The 1928 construction of the O'Dell Apartments (which would later become the Sierra Grande Lodge) coincided with a national trend in automobile tourism in the United States. The town of Hot Springs lured tourists as well as turberculosis patients with the therapeutic values of mineral baths and a clear, dry climate. When the O'Dell Apartments began to attract tourists and health seekers, the building was converted to the O'Dell Hotel. The hotel had a professional masseur who managed the hotel's mineral baths. By the late 1940s, social trends favored western medicine and deemphasized traditional healing methods, and the town faded. Around this time, the building became known as the Sierra Grande Lodge. The lodge is a two-story painted stucco building in downtown Truth or Consequences. It occupies a full city block and is known locally as the Grand Hotel. The building has two water systems, one domestic and the other mineral; the latter comes to the surface at 105 degrees and is recycled back into the town's mineral water system.

Tyrone *(Grant County)*

Burro Springs Site No. 2 (LA 11609)

SR #314 (1974), NR #74001197 (1974)

Vado *(Doña Ana County)*

Valley Grove Baptist Church

221 Holguin Rd.

SR #1607 (1994)

Winston *(Socorro County)*

Ojo Caliente Military Post (LA 3947)

SR #512 (1977)

Southeast

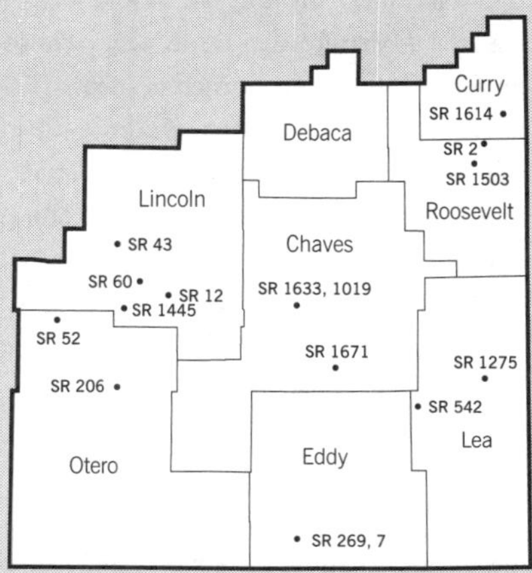

Though the Southeastern region contains the high, forested Capitan and Sacramento Mountains and the rugged Guadalupes, most of southeastern New Mexico consists of a vast desert landscape, dotted with cactus and succulents, rolling down from the mountains to the Pecos River then up again to join the *Llano Estacado,* the Staked Plains stretching through west Texas. At the beginning of human history in the New World, this land was home to the roving bands of Paleoindians, who left their beautifully worked stone tools mixed with the bones of the huge Ice Age animals that they hunted. Subsequently southeastern New Mexico was occupied for millennia by groups of hunters and gatherers who made a successful living from buffalo and smaller game, acorns and roasted hearts of the various species of succulent agaves. In early historic times the southeast was home to the Mescalero Apache and visited by the Kiowa, Comanche and other nomadic tribes of the Southern Plains. Though small groups of Hispanic settlers colonized the far western part of this region, Euroamerican settlement of most of the southeast began with the influx of Texas cattlemen after the Civil War, swelled in the last quarter of the 19th century by land and water development schemes and homesteading, and boomed in the mid 20th century with oil and gas development. National and State Register listings in the southeast range from ancient Paleoindian hunting sites to the first oil well in southeastern New Mexico, and from sites associated with the overplayed villains of the Lincoln County War to sites associated with the unsung heroes of hardscrabble homesteads and ranches.

Alamogordo *(Otero County)*

Harry Francis Ackley House
1115 Indiana Ave.
SR #1210 (1985)

Administration Building (NMSVH)
1900 N. White Sands Blvd.
SR #1473 (1988), NR #88001564 (1989),
☒ 1707

Alamo Springs Stage Station (LA 9076)
Near Alamo Mountain
SR #172 (1970)

Auditorium and Recreation Building (NMSVH)
1900 N. White Sands Blvd.
SR #1474 (191988), NR #88001565 (1989),
☒ 1707

Central Receiving Building (NMSVH)
1900 N. White Sands Blvd.
SR #1475 (1988), NR #88001566 (1989),
☒ 1707

Infirmary Building (NMSVH)
1900 N. White Sands Blvd.
SR #1476 (1988), NR #88001567 (1989),
☒ 1707

Parabolic Dune Hearth Mounds
In White Sands National Monument
SR #434 (1976)

E.P. Rees House
1325 Indiana Ave.
SR #1211 (1985)

Charlie Thomas House
1303 Ohio Ave.
SR #1690 (1997)

White Sands National Monument Historic District
US 70/82
SR #1491 (1988), NR #88000751 (1988)

Alto *(Lincoln County)*

Monjeau Lookout
Lincoln National Forest, Madonna Peak
SR #1445 (1988), NR #87002483 (1988),
☒ 1708

The National Forests of New Mexico were created mainly between 1892 and 1907. A major focus of the Forest Service was, and still is, fire management. In the early part of the 20th century, fire protection strategies including rapid detection of fires from

lookout posts were implemented. The Monjeau Lookout is located in the Lincoln National Forest in the Smokey Bear Ranger District, the same area where Smokey Bear, a badly burned bear cub who lived to become a national symbol of forest fire prevention, was rescued in 1950. The lookout was built in 1940 with labor and funding from the Civilian Conservation Corps (CCC), a New Deal agency. It was an observation-only lookout tower with a 7-by-7-foot metal cab manufactured by International Derrick, built on a 14-by-14-foot tower of native stone. In a unique configuration, the living quarters are located below the cab in the stone tower. The lookout is illustrated in the *Forest Service Standard Lookout Planbook* orginally published in 1938 and is an excellent example of "Rustic Style" construction often used by the CCC in National Park Service and Forest Service buildings. The Monjeau and other lookouts are symbols of America's forest system and forest conservation policy.

Ancho *(Lincoln County)*

Ancho Railroad Depot (Building)
Off NM 54
SR #399 (1975)

Artesia *(Eddy County)*

John Acord House
801 W. Main St.
SR #997 (1983), NR #84002891 (1984),
☒ 1702

Willie D. Atkeson House
303 W. Grand Ave.
SR #999(1983), NR #84002894 (1984),
☒ 1702

Baskin Building
332 W. Main St.
SR #1372 (1987), NR #90000599 (1990)

William Baskin House
811 W. Quay Ave.
SR #995 (1983), NR #84002898 (1984), ⊠ 1702

Flynn/Welch/Yates No. 3 Oil Well
Oil City Road
SR #1410 (1988)

Edward R. Gesler House
411 W. Missouri Ave.
SR #996 (1983), NR #84002924 (1984), ⊠ 1702

Hodges/Runyan/Brainard House
504 W. Quay Ave.
SR #994 (1983), NR #84002925 (1984), ⊠ 1702

Hodges/Sipple House
804 W. Missouri Ave.
SR #998 (1983), NR #84002926 (1984), ⊠ 1702

F.L. Lukins House
801 W. Richardson Ave.
SR #993 (1983), NR #84002928 (1984), ⊠ 1702

Mauldin/Hall House
501 S. Roselawn Ave.
SR #1001 (1983), NR #84002930 (1984), ⊠ 1702

Moore/Ward Cobblestone House
505 W. Richardson Ave.
SR #447 (1976), NR #84002932 (1984)

Sallie Chisum Robert House
801 W. Texas St.
SR #515 (1977), NR #84002939 (1984), ⊠ 1702

Dr. Robert M. Ross House
1002 S. Roselawn Ave.
SR #1000 (1983), NR #84002936 (1984), ⊠ 1702

Sipple/Ward Building
331 W. Main St.
SR #1537 (1991), NR #91001503 (1991)

Capitan *(Lincoln County)*

Capitan Depot
NM 48 and NM 380
SR #697 (1978)

Fort Stanton
Near U.S. 380
SR #60 (1969), NR #73001142 (1973)

Fort Stanton was established in 1855 to control attacks by the nomadic Mescalero Apaches living in southeastern New Mexico; it was named after Captain Henry Stanton, who had been killed in a skirmish with the Mescaleros earlier that year. The fort's shingle-roofed, stone buildings were laid out around a large, rectangular parade ground. Other facilities included corrals and two cemeteries. During the Civil War, Union forces abandoned the fort when New Mexico was invaded by Confederate forces, but Colonel Kit Carson and his New Mexico Cavalry reoccupied it a year later. The fort was subsequently the center of continuous hostilities with the Mescalero Apache Indians, who finally agreed to settle on a reservation in 1871. The fort was an important cash market for supplies for the fort and for the reservation in the 1870s; the struggle to control this market was an aspect of the Lincoln County War. The post was officially abandoned in 1896, and less than three years later the facility became the first Federal hospital exclusively for the treatment of tuberculosis. Used as a hospital for

the developmentally disabled until a few years ago, it was most recently a women's correctional facility. Fort Stanton, with twelve buildings dating prior to 1896 and several others that retain features of the original pre-Civil War permanent structures, is one of the best-preserved forts of the period of the Indian Wars in the American West.

Los Patos Ruins (LA 66358)
On Patos Creek
SR #662 (1978)

Caprock *(Chaves County)*

Causey Ranch House
SR #360 (1975)

Mescalero Sands Archaelogical District
SR #433 (1976)

Mescalero Sands Site (LA 2525)
SR #160 (1970), MESCALERO SANDS ARCHAEOLOGICAL DISTRICT

Carlsbad *(Eddy County)*

Carlsbad Caverns National Park Historic District
NM 7
SR #269 (1973), NR #88001173 (1988)

Apache people knew about the Carlsbad Caverns and named the natural entrance "bats fly out at night." In 1901 James Larkin White, a young cowboy, mistook the emerging bats for trails of smoke and went to investigate, finding a vast network of caverns beneath the surface. The site was subsequently mined for bat guano, a rich fertilizer, and in 1923, Carlsbad Caverns National Monument was created. Early visitors entered the cave in a steel bucket suspended on metal cables. The historic district at Carlsbad Caverns consists of a group of thirteen National Park headquarters buildings and landscaped features near the natural entrance to the cave, built in the 1920s, 1930s and 1940s by the National Park Service and, later,

by CCC construction crews. The eight limestone buildings built from 1926 to 1932 are in the Pueblo Revival style, imitating the broken masonry of prehistoric structures, while four buildings from the 1940s are Territorial Style adobes. The buildings exemplify the "rustic" theme used in facility development during the early years of the National Park System.

Carlsbad Reclamation Project District ▲
SR #7 (1968), NR #66000476 (1966)

The Carlsbad Irrigation District is a reclamation system in the Pecos River Valley near the community of Carlsbad (known as Eddy until 1899) which provides irriga-

tion water to about 25,000 acres of farmland. It includes McMillan Dam and its reservoir, spillways, embankments and railroad dikes; Avalon Dam and its reservoir, spillways, suspension bridge, gatekeeper's house and other structures; as well as canals, flumes, siphons and supply ditches; and its headquarters, the First National Bank of Eddy, an Italianate commercial business block built in 1890. This project was originally a private enterprise, the Pecos Irrigation and Investment Company, formed by Charles B. Eddy and Pat Garrett (former Lincoln County sheriff). The Company built Avalon Dam and McMillan Dam in the early 1890s, but lapsed into bankruptcy in 1898 and was eventually reorganized. In 1905 it was taken over by the federal Reclamation Service, created in 1902 to provide for irrigation in the arid West on a scale impossible for private entrepreneurs. Water storage was supplemented by the construction of Alamogordo (now Fort Sumner) Dam in 1938 and the completion of Brantley Dam in 1988. The Carlsbad Irrigation District represents the history of western American reclamation activity. It may be the best example in the West of the evolution from a private irrigation enterprise to federal control.

Rattlesnake Springs Historic District
CR 418
SR #1496 (1989) NR #88001130 (1988)

Painted Grotto (LA 46313)
SR #498 (1977), NR #77000159 (1977), CARLSBAD CAVERNS NATIONAL PARK HISTORIC DISTRICT

Eddy & Bissell Livestock Company Headquarters
SR #280 (1973)

Eddy County Courthouse
200 block of W. Mermond
SR #1277 (1986), ☒ 1722

Eddy National Bank
303 W. Fox St.
SR #208 (1971), NR #76001196 (1976)

J.J. Hagerman House
Greene St.
SR #472 (1976)

Lake Avalon
Pecos River
SR #557 (1978)

Lusk Ranch Site (LA 43721)
SR #159 (1970)

Phenix Adobe (LA 43457)
Sonora St. and Railroad Ave.
SR #474 (1976)

Pope's Wells Site (Los Lentes Pueblo) (LA 4978)
SR #240 (1972)

Carrizozo *(Lincoln County)*

Robert Olinger's Wallet
Lincoln County Courthouse
SR #1411 (1988)

Cloudcroft *(Otero County)*

Cloudcroft Lodge
Corona Place
SR #1407 (1987)

Cloudcroft Municipal School
Burro Ave. and Swallow Pl.
SR #1498 (1989)

Hubbell Canyon Log Chute
SR #1754, NR #91001882 (1991), ☒ 1730

Mexican Canyon (Cloudcroft) Railroad Trestle
SR #206 (1970), NR #79001543 (1979)

The town of Cloudcroft was founded by Charles Eddy, who constructed the Alamogordo and Sacramento Mountain Railway in 1899 to 1900 to bring timber from the Sacramento Mountains to his El Paso and Northeastern Railroad. The Sacramento Mountain area was rich in timber and logging, as in other areas of New Mexico, became an important industry. Cloudcroft, with its cool summer temperatures, became a popular tourist destination, particularly with Texans; the dramatic 4,500-foot climb by train included grades of 6.4%, a switchback and 58 trestles on its 32-mile route. Passenger service ended in 1938 and the lumber company's shift to the use of motor trucks caused the end of freight service in 1947. The rails were removed in 1948 and the depot was demolished in 1949. The Mexican Trestle is the most prominent structure remaining from one of New Mexico's most spectacular railroads. The Mexican Canyon (Cloudcroft) Trestle, built in 1899, was one of the 58 trestles on the "cloud-climbing railroad." The curved structure is 323 feet long and rises 52 feet above the canyon floor. Its vertical supports, spaced 15 feet apart, consist of 12-by-12-inch timbers. The rails and crossties were placed on 8-by-16-inch stringers held together with three-quarter inch bolts and cast iron spacers. To form the curve, the stringers were built in 21 sections. Lateral, longitudinal and diagonal wooden braces prevented sway and shifting of the trestle. A trail from a reconstruction of the old railroad depot leads to the edge of the trestle, but walking on the structure is not permitted.

Springville (Kent Ecton Kabin)
Corona St. and Otter St.
SR #1518 (1990)

Wills Canyon Spur Trestle
SR #1753, NR #91001881 (1991), ☒ 1730

Wofford Lookout Complex
Lincoln National Forest
SR #1446 (1988), NR #87002484 (1988), ☒ 1708

Clovis *(Curry County)*

Clovis City Hall and Fire Station – 1908
308 Pile St.
SR #1380 (1987), NR #87001110 (1987)

Clovis Baptist Hospital
515 Prince St.
SR #837 (1981), NR #82003322 (1982)

Clovis Central Fire Station
320 Mitchell St.
SR #1381(1987), NR #87001111 (1987)

Curry County Courthouse
700 block of Main St.
SR #1274 (1986), NR #87000881 (1987), ☒ 1722

Dr. Fred A. Dillon House
1400 Axtell St.
SR #1488 (1988)

First Methodist Church of Clovis
622 Main St.
SR #1379 (1987), NR #87001112 (1987)

Hotel Clovis
210 Main St.
SR #1109 (1984), NR #84000571 (1984)

Old Clovis Post Office
4th St. and Mitchell St.
SR #1108 (1984), NR #84000573 (1984)

Santa Fe Passenger Depot, Clovis
221 W. 1st St.
SR #1614 (1995), NR #95001451 (1995)

In 1908 the Eastern Railway of New Mexico, a subsidiary of the Atchison, Topeka and Santa Fe Railroad, built the "Belen Cutoff" to connect Texas with the West Coast. The division point where the line from Pecos, Texas, joins the Belen Cutoff was named "Riley's Switch" by the railroad, but the new town was named Clovis by the chief engineer's daughter who was reading French history and admired the French king. The railroad depot and division office at Clovis was built in 1908. It is typical of Eastern Railway depots; all were similar Mission Style buildings constructed of concrete with a stucco finish, red tile roofs and extended roof overhangs with arched supports. The depot was a passenger depot until 1971, when Amtrak took over rail passenger service in the U.S. When passenger service along the line ceased in 1989, the building was abandoned by the railroad. The Clovis depot has not been significantly altered. Currently the home of a model train museum, it still looks out over an active railyard in a town that owes its existence, like many towns in New Mexico, to the railroad.

Fort Sumner *(De Baca County)*

De Baca County Courthouse
500 block of Ave. C
SR #1270 (1986), NR #87000896 (1987),
⊠ 1722

Fort Sumner Railroad Bridge
Over Pecos River
SR #551 (1978), NR #79001539 (1979)

Fort Sumner State Monument (Fort Sumner Ruins) (LA 8777)
SR #139 (1970), NR #74001194 (1974)

Rodrick Drug Store
505 Main St.
SR #435 (1976)

Hagerman *(Chaves County)*

First Hagerman School House
210 N. Winchester Ave.
SR #1377 (1987)

Rio Felix Bridge at Hagerman
NM 2 over Rio Felix
SR #1671 (1997), NR #97000737 (1997),
⊠ 1661

During the 1920s, the highway department sought to complete the first phase

of the state's modern road system by connecting the principal communities of the state. This was the beginning a state program to construct permanent bridges over rivers and drainages. The Rio Felix Bridge, located north of Hagerman on the former alignment of New Mexico Highway 2, is a three-span steel structure fabricated by the Boardman Company of Oklahoma City in 1926. The bridge incorporates a Pratt through truss with rigid connections. Each of the three 144-foot long spans is composed of eight eighteen-foot-long panels. Since the road aligns with section lines, it crosses the Rio Felix at an angle. However, for stability during flooding, the concrete piers supporting the bridge were placed parallel to the flow line of the river. As a solution, the panels of each span are offset one panel length to permit the spans to rest on these piers. The bridge was bypassed in 1984 but was preserved by the Highway Department at the request of the Historic Preservation Division. The Rio Felix Bridge is the state's oldest and longest Pratt through-truss bridge with rigid connections and a reminder of the development of New Mexico's modern road system.

Rio Feliz Bridge
SR 2
SR #573 (1978)

High Rolls *(Otero County)*

Fresnal Shelter (Alamogordo Site) (LA 10101)
SR #152 (1970), ⊠ 1755

High Rolls/Mountain Park Methodist Church
Haynes Canyon
SR #702 (1978)

Hobbs *(Lea County)*

Laguna Plata Archaeological District
SR #1520 (1990), NR #89001209 (1989)

Jicarilla *(Lincoln County)*

Jicarilla Schoolhouse
NM 349
SR #524 (1977), NR #83001623 (1983)

La Luz *(Otero County)*

Juan Garcia House
Tularosa St.
SR #1287 (1979), NR #80002559 (1980), ⊠ 720

Juan Jose Gutierrez House
SR #411 (1975), LA LUZ TOWNSITE HISTORIC DISTRICT

La Luz Pottery Factory

SR #708 (1978), NR #79001544 (1979)

La Luz Townsite Historic District

Main St. and Sacramento St.

SR #720 (1979), NR #80002560 (1980), ☒ 720

Queen Anne House

Kearny St.

SR #1289 (1979), NR #80002561 (1980), ☒ 720

D. H. Sutherland House (Ramirez House)

Main St.

SR #1288 (1979), NR #80002562 (1980), ☒ 720

Lincoln *(Lincoln County)*

Double Crossing Ruin (LA 12151)

SR #1477 (1988), NR #88001507 (1988), ☒ 1706

Feather Cave (LA 37551)

SR #156 (1970), NR #74001198 (1974)

Former Lincoln County Courthouse in Lincoln

Southwest side of US 380

SR #1263 (1986), LINCOLN HISTORIC DISTRICT, ☒ 1722

Hondo Project (LA 5380)

SR #554 (1978)

LA 12153

SR #1478 (1988), NR #88001508 (1990), ☒ 1706

LA 12155

SR #1479 (1988), NR #88001509 (1990), ☒ 1706

LA 61200

SR #1480 (1988), ☒ 1706

LA 61201

SR #1481 (1988), NR #88001510 (1988), ☒ 1706

LA 61202

SR #1482 (1988), NR #88001511 (1990), ☒ 1706

LA 61204

SR #1483 (1988), NR #88001512 (1988), ☒ 1706

LA 61208

SR #1485 (1988), NR #88001514 (1988), ☒ 1706

LA 61210

SR #1486 (1988), NR #88001516 (1988), ☒ 1706

LA 61211

SR #1487 (1988), NR #88001515 (1988), ☒ 1706

Lincoln Historic District ▲

US 380

SR #12 (1968), NR #66000477 (1966)

Lincoln, originally *La Placita del Rio Bonito,* "the little town of the beautiful river," was founded about 1854 by Hispanic farmers from the Rio Grande Valley, who took advantage of U.S. military protection from the Apaches to farm these fertile lands. In 1873 there were about 100 people in the town, with only one Anglo family. By 1880 there were sixty structures including

the Murphy-Dolan Store (old county courthouse), built in 1874, and the Tunstall-McSween Store, built in 1878. Lincoln was the focus of the Lincoln County War of 1878, in which the rival Murphy-Dolan and Tunstall-McSween factions fought for control of southeastern New Mexico's new ranching economy. The War eventually involved John S. Chisum, the region's greatest cattle baron; Lew Wallace, territorial governor and author of *Ben Hur,* who was forced to intervene; and William H. Bonney, a young cowboy of the Tunstall-McSween interests who, as Billy the Kid, became the most famous of all Western outlaws. Lincoln is perhaps the best preserved example in the entire West of a frontier cow town.

Rancho Torres (LA 61206)

SR #1484 (1988), NR #88001513 (1988), ⊠ 1706

Loving *(Eddy County)*

Original Potash Bullwheel

SR #567 (1978)

Lovington *(Lea County)*

Lea County Courthouse

100 block of Main St.

SR #1275 (1986), NR #87000880 (1987), ⊠ 1722

Pueblo Revival became the predominant style in New Mexico in the 1930s. Among the relatively few Art Deco structures from this period are six county courthouses, including the 1936 Lea County Courthouse, designed by O.R. Walker. The courthouse is a three-story, rectangular blond brick building with bas-relief embellishment, situated on a Shelbyville-type court square that is the center of Lovington. The building has two sections: a central section of three stories and a two-story wing surrounding the building on three sides. This configuration gives the courthouse a stepped, symmetrical front facade. The concrete bas relief panels that connect the third-story windows are decorated in an abstract Indian motif. The entrance is reached by two short flights of stairs, flanked by Art Deco light standards and metal handrails. The interior is detailed with terrazzo flooring, marble wainscoting and plaster walls. The exterior frontispiece has a thunder-

bird motif that is repeated in the foyer in ceramic tile. The Lea County Courthouse blends Southwestern and Maya genres of Art Deco ornamentation with the formal Classicism that was popular in public architecture in the 1930s. It is one of the best Art Deco buildings in New Mexico.

Pyburn House and Associated Structures

203 N. 4th St.

SR #1593 (1994), NR #95001429 (1995)

Maljamar *(Lea County)*

Baish Oil Well No. 1

SR #542 (1978)

The first report of oil in New Mexico occurred in 1882, when a prospecting

party discovered a flowing well near the Navajo Reservation in San Juan County. Commercial production began there in 1922 and in Lea County in 1924. The Baish Oil Well Number One, named for field superintendent Mel Baish of Artesia, was the first oil-producing well in Lea County (following earlier operations in the Artesia area); it began a trend that has made Lea County the leading producer of oil in New Mexico. The well, a standard cable tool rig with an 84-foot derrick, was drilled by Maljamar Oil and Gas Corporation and began to produce in 1925. The cable rig drilled percussively, by raising and dropping a heavy steel bit with a chisel end suspended on a steel cable. A walking beam transmitted the vertical motion to the drill bit. A single-cylinder gasoline engine transmitted power from a belt pulley to a bandwheel, which then turned a pitman, transferring energy from a rotary motion to a vertical action. The engine was housed in a sheet-iron wood frame shed. This percussion system of drilling has since been abandoned in favor of the more precise rotary method. The Baish Oil Well No. 1 produced until 1969, and was then converted into a repressuring input well designed for secondary recovery in the Maljamar Pool. All that now remains of the well are cement foundations and a pressure valve. This well, although never more than a minor producer, is significant as a memorial to the emergence of a major industry.

Burro Tanks Site (LA 32227)
(in Chaves County)
SR #155 (1970)

Rattlesnake Draw Site (LA 5146)
SR #167 (1970)

Red Tank (Boot Hill) Archaeological Site (LA 32229) *(in Eddy County)*
SR #168 (1970)

Taylor Peak Site (LA 32228)
SR #171 (1970)

Mayhill *(Otero County)*

C-A Bar Ranch House (James Fielding Hinkle House) *(in Chaves County)*
US 82 west of junction with NM 24
SR #1015 (1984), NR #85003634 (1988), ⊠ 1649

Mayhill Administrative Site Archaeological District (LA 505)
US 82
SR #1504, NR #89000476 (1989)

Hay Canyon Logging Camp
SR #1752, NR #91001880 (1992), ⊠ 1730

Mescalero *(Otero County)*

Wally's Dome
SR #855 (1982)

Monument *(Lea County)*

Monument Springs Site (LA 43256)
SR #162 (1970)

Nogal *(Lincoln County)*

Aguayo Family Homestead
Tortolita Canyon
SR #1747, NR #95001478 (1995), ☒ 1712

Bonito Pipeline (El Paso and Southwestern Railway Water Supply System) (LA 16488)
NM 37
SR #544 (1978), NR #79001540 (1979)

Hopeful Lode (Parson's Mine) (LA 31784)
FR 108
SR #1598 (1994), NR #95001014 (1995), ☒ 1597

Mesa Ranger Station Site (LA 66281)
SR #1743, NR #90001533 (1990), ☒ 1729

Nogal Mesa Kiva Site
SR #1742, NR #90001532 (1990), ☒ 1729

Nogal Mesa Site (LA 35030)
SR #1741, NR #90001531 (1990), ☒ 1729

Orogrande *(Otero County)*

Escondido Ruin (LA 458)
SR #99 (1969)

Grapevine Canyon Archaeological District
SR #765 (1980)

Picacho *(Lincoln County)*

Rio Hondo Bridge at Picacho
CR A-4
SR #1668 (1997), ☒ 1661

Portales *(Roosevelt County)*

Administration Building (ENMU)
South of University Pl. and campus green
SR #1468 (1988), NR #88001558 (1988), ☒ 1707

Anderson Basin (Blackwater Draw) (LA 3324) ▲
SR #2 (1968), NR #66000483 (1966)

Blackwater Draw is the remains of an extinct riverbed running from the Sangre de Cristo Mountains of New Mexico to the Brazos River in Texas. During the Late Pleistocene era, the Pecos River cut this drainage, creating ephemeral streams, spring-fed lakes and natural catch-basins which were of great importance to the area's inhabitants. The property consists of two separate localities, Locality No. 1 (commonly called the Clovis Site) and Locality No. 2 (also called Anderson Basin). The people called Clovis hunted mammoth and bison here about 11,500 years ago. After the mammoths died out about 11,000 years ago, the people called Folsom hunted bison up to about 10,200 years ago. The change from Clovis to Folsom tool technology may simply reflect a change in the type of animal that was hunted. Blackwater Draw has yielded large numbers of Clovis and Folsom artifacts in association with extinct Pleistocene animals, and is one of the nation's most important early man (Paleoindian) sites. There is a small visitor center and a trail that leads from

the center to a building (constructed using money appropriated by the New Mexico legislature to the Historic Preservation Division) housing archaeological excavations in progress.

Bank of Portales
123 Main St.
SR #1111 (1984), NR #84000635 (1984)

Portales Main Post Office
116 W. 1st St.
SR #106, NR #90000140 (1990), ☒ 1704

Portales Woman's Club
309 W. 1st St.
SR #1503 (1989)

The Portales Woman's Club was the first women's organization in Roosevelt County, founded in 1903 to promote enhanced community life in Portales, including good schools, a community library, social activities for families, churches and beautification projects. The 1400 square foot Territorial Style building was designed by Robert Merrill, one of the first architects licensed in New Mexico, and was completed in 1932. Nineteen *vigas* (ceiling beams) extend from the facade and east end of the building. It has hardwood floors, a gas fireplace and a large wooden mantel and mirror at the front of the meeting room. A pitched roof was added in 1977 to stop leaks in the original flat roof. The building continues to provide a permanent site for the headquarters of Portales Woman's Club and also serves as a gathering place for the community of Portales. It represents a vision of progressive community life in an area of recent settlement.

Roosevelt County Courthouse
100 W. 2nd St.
SR #1278 (1986), ☒ 1722

Queen *(Eddy County)*

Dam (Sitting Bull Falls Recreation Area)
Lincoln National Forest
SR #1740, NR #93001420 (1993), ☒ 1737

Group Picnic Shelter (Sitting Bull Falls Recreation Area)
Lincoln National Forest
SR #1739, NR #93001419 (1993), ☒ 1737

LA 67073
SR #1745, NR #95001320 (1995), ☒ 1731

LA 64952
SR #1744, NR #95001319 (1995), ☒ 1731

LA 28702 *(in Otero County)*
SR #1746, NR #95001479 (1995), ☒ 1731

Picnic Shelter (Sitting Bull Falls Recreation Area)
Lincoln National Forest
SR #1738, NR #93001418 (1993), ☒ 1737

Roswell *(Chaves County)*

Chihuahuita Historic District
Bounded by Brown St., the Rio Hondo, Garden Ave., Tilden St., Elm Ave.
SR #1007 (1984), ☒ 1649

Conoco Service Station
426 N. Main St.
SR #1633 (1996)

Trails and roads have played a major role in the development of southeastern New Mexico. Prehistoric traders created trails

across the Llano Estacado and up and down the Pecos River. The east-west trails created by the comancheros, traders to the Comanches and other Plains people, were later used by Anglo trading and military expeditions. And the Goodnight-Loving cattle trail extended through the southeast part of the state through Santa Fe to Colorado. The earliest automobile roads in Chaves County appeared around 1900, usually following old trails, stage routes and railroads. The automobile led to the development of many highway-associated resources such as motels, diners, cafes, rest stops, billboards and, of course, filling stations, a new building type. The roadside businesses competed for the attention of the traveler through the design of their buildings and with standardized symbols and signs. Conoco adopted a residential style for its familiarity and inviting scale. The Conoco Service Station in Roswell, reminiscent of the residential Tudor Revival style popular in the first half of the 20th century, is a 46-by-26-foot rectangular building with a steeply pitched gable roof, a plank wood front entry door with decorative hinges and a decorative chimney. The station originally had service bays reached through the overhead garage-style doors. Though the doors remain, the station is now a visitor center and the offices of the Hispano Chamber of Commerce, which has remodeled the building and removed the gas pumps.

Diamond A Ranch House and Bunkhouse
US 380
SR #1014 (1984), NR #85003635 (1988), ☒ 1649

Dilley/Ballard Mortuary
121 W. 3rd St.
SR #1652 (1997), ☒ 1649

Downtown Roswell Historic District
Bounded by Hill St., Richardson Ave., Albuquerque St. and Missouri Ave.
SR #1006 (1984), NR #85001543 (1985), ☒ 1649

Bill and Birdie Dee Eccles Farmhouse
3754 E. Grand Plains Rd.
SR #1655 (1997), ☒ 1649

Flying H Ranch
North of US 82 between Hope and Elk
SR #1009 (1984), NR #85003633 (1988), ☒ 1649

Patrick Floyd Garrett House
Bosque Rd.
SR #1011 (1984), NR #85003637 (1988), ☒ 1649

Robert H. Goddard House
1501 E. Mescalero Rd.
SR #1021 (1984), NR #85003594 (1988), ☒ 1649

Goddard Rocket Collection, Roswell Museum
100 W. 11th St.
SR #148 (1970)

Louise Massey House
209 W. Alameda St.
SR #1020 (1984), NR #85001544 (1985), ☒ 1649

Millhiser/Baker Farmhouse
Wyoming St.
SR #1016 (1984), NR #85003638 (1988), ☒ 1649

Milne/Bush Ranch, Ranch House and Barn

SR #1013 (1984), NR #85003639 (1988), ☒ 1649

New Mexico Military Institute Historic District

Bounded by 19th St., N. Main St., College Blvd. and Kentucky Ave.

SR #1008 (1984), NR #87000907 (1987), ☒ 1649

Milo L. and Ella Lea Calfee Pierce House

1303 E. Poe St.

SR #1650 (1997), ☒ 1649

Old Presbyterian Parsonage

208 N. Michigan Ave.

SR #1651 (1997), ☒ 1649

'Judge' George L. Reese, Jr. House

712 W. Alameda St.

SR #1653 (1997), ☒ 1649

Roswell – Chaves County Courthouse

400 Blk. Main St.

SR #1019 (1984), NR #87000892 (1989), ☒ 1649, ☒ 1722

Chaves County, created by the Territorial Legislature in 1899, was carved out of enormous Lincoln County, which covered the whole southeast quarter of New Mexico.

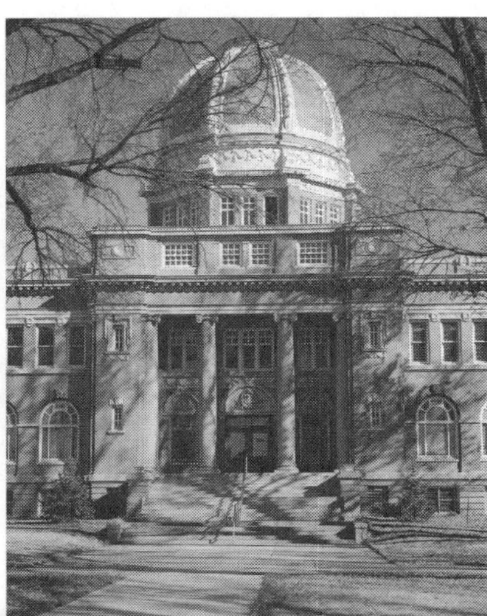

Roswell, the largest settlement in the area with 354 people, became the county seat. The Chaves County Courthouse in Roswell was designed by Isaac Hamilton Rapp of I.H. and W.M. Rapp in Colorado, prominent architects who were responsible for public buildings across the country including the New Mexico Territorial Capitol and the Governor's Mansion. The building is a rare example in New Mexico of Beaux-Arts influenced styling and of a courthouse built in a monumental scale. The yellow-brick building, completed in 1911, is typical of Beaux-Arts styling with a strictly symmetrical five-part facade organized around a dominant central entrance and a strong Classical cornice. Its most prominent feature is the green-tiled dome on an eight-sided concrete base supported by eight-sided brick walls. The interior is built around a central domed lobby open to the first and second floors. The yellow brick jail, including the sheriff's dwelling, was constructed at the same time in a simpler, yet complementary style. It has been connected to the courthouse by additions in 1954 and 1974.

Saunders/Crosby House

200 E. Deming

SR #1018 (1984), NR #85001545 (1985), ☒ 1649

Slaughter/Hill Ranch Log House (Cunningham Homestead)

1601 E. 2nd St.

SR #1012 (1984), NR #85003640 (1988), ☒ 1649

South Spring Ranch Outbuildings

SR #1010 (1984), NR #88003465 (1989), ☒ 1649

Tweedy Family Farmhouse

5606 Old Dexter Highway

SR #1656 (1997), ☒ 1649

Urton Orchards Farmhouse and Milkhouse
SR #1017 (1984), NR #85003641 (1988), ☒ 1649

J.P. and Lou T. White House
200 N. Lea Ave.
SR #425 (1976), NR #78001812 (1978), DOWNTOWN ROSWELL HISTORIC DISTRICT

J.P. White, Jr. House
212 N. Missouri Ave.
SR #1654 (1997), ☒ 1649

Seven Rivers *(Eddy County)*

Lake McMillan Dam
SR #558 (1978)

Seven Rivers
SR #77 (1969)

Ruidoso *(Otero County)*

A.B. Fall Dam and Aqueduct
SR #585 (1978)

New Mexico Military Institute Summer Camp, Main Building
Carrizo Canyon
SR #838 (1981), NR #83001622 (1983)

Ruidoso Lookout Tower
North of NM 37
SR #1447 (1988), NR #87002485 (1988), ☒ 1708

Wizard's Roost (LA 29588)
SR #845 (1981), NR #82004841 (1982)

Sacramento *(Otero County)*

Circle Cross Ranch Main House
SR #775 (1980), NR #80002553 (1980)

Weed Lookout Tower
Lincoln National Forest
SR #1449 (1988), NR #87002487 (1988), ☒ 1708

Texico *(Curry County)*

Atchison, Topeka & Santa Fe Railway Depot
Highway 70
SR #727 (1979)

Three Rivers *(Otero County)*

Three Rivers Petroglyph and Pueblo Site (LA 4921)
SR #52 (1969)

People of the Jornada branch of the Mogollon culture occupied the Three Rivers area from around A.D. 900 to around A.D. 1300. They moved into the area from the west and lived in a pithouse village 300 yards from the Three Rivers ridge. Their petroglyphs, figures carved with stone tools on black volcanic rock, lie along a ridgetop in the upper reaches of the northeast Tularosa Basin. The ridge, with vast views of the Sierra Blanca to the east and the Basin to the west, was a good vantage point for observing game or enemies. The petroglyphs cover an area of about 40 acres and include

drawings of game, sunbursts, footprints, handprints, faces and various geometric designs. The site is open to the public with a trail that winds up the hillside so visitors can view the numerous petroglyphs.

Tinnie *(Lincoln County)*

Rio Hondo Bridge
NM 399
SR #744 (1979)

Tularosa *(Otero County)*

Tularosa Original Townsite District
US 54/70
SR #703 (1978), NR #79001545 (1979)

Weed *(Otero County)*

Bluewater Lookout Complex
Lincoln National Forest
SR #1448 (1988), NR #87002486 (1988), ☒ 1708

Carrisa Lookout Complex
Lincoln National Forest
SR #1450 (1988), NR #87002488 (1988), ☒ 1708

White Oaks *(Lincoln County)*

Funston Site (LA 61196)
SR #1748, NR #90001250 (1990), ☒ 1710

LA 61198
SR #1749, NR #90001251 (1990), ☒ 1710

Sandy Tank Site (LA 51336)
SR #1750, NR #90001252 (1990), ☒ 1710

White Oaks Historic District
NM 349
SR #43 (1969), NR #70000403 (1970)

The White Oaks Historic District includes the ghost town of White Oaks and its associated mining area around Baxter Mountain. Mining took place as early as 1850, but the rich lodes, such as North and South Homestakes, were located in 1879. Gold was the most important metal, but the mines also yielded deposits of silver, lead, copper, iron and tungsten. The mines had colorful names such as Old Abe (the richest vein in the field), Yellow Jacket, Rip Van Winkle, Lady Godiva, Boston Boy, and Large Hopes. The town of White Oaks is about a mile and a half from the mining area; it once boasted a sawmill, two banks, three churches, an opera house, a schoolhouse, four newspapers, at least eight gambling halls, numerous stores, saloons, and brothels. Confident of continued growth and prosperity, local businessmen demanded high prices for property yet failed to court the El Paso and Northeastern Railroad. When it bypassed White Oaks in favor of Carrizozo in 1899, the town began to decline. Remaining structures in the town include the schoolhouse, the shell of the Exchange Bank, the stone Hoyle House, some smaller buildings and the Cedarvale cemetery. Remaining mining structures include several headframes and hoist machinery.

Roads, Trails and Routes

The earlier roads, trails and routes that crossed New Mexico later became the basis for the territory's railroads, then state highways and interstates. The earliest roads were trade routes such as the Santa Fe Trail, established in 1821 as a trade route between Santa Fe and the eastern United States, and the Camino Real, the trade route between Santa Fe and cities in Mexico. Stagecoach roads were introduced in 1849, and by 1882 there were 38 separate lines. Most were north-south roads; the Butterfield Overland Mail Route, however, was an east-west road which ran through Apache country in the southern part of the state. Military wagon roads were developed to connect military forts, established to control Indians, with nearby towns. Cattle drives began in 1866 after the Civil War. Cattle trails included the Goodnight/Loving Trail, which extended from the southeast part of the state through Santa Fe to Colorado, and the Magdalena Stock Driveway.

Butterfield Overland Mail Route
SR #173 (1970)

El Camino Real
SR #174 (1970)

Goodnight/Loving Trail
SR #175 (1970)

High Road to Taos
SR #363 (1975)

Magdalena Stock Driveway
SR #299 (1973)

Pecos River Route (Espejo and Castaño de Sosa)
SR #178 (1970)

Raton to Santa Fe Stage Route
SR #180 (1970)

Santa Fe Trail
SR #183 (1970)

Santa Fe to El Paso Stage Route
SR #181 (1970)

Santa Fe to Prescott Stage Route
SR #182 (1970)

Zuni/Rio Grande Trail
SR #184 (1970)

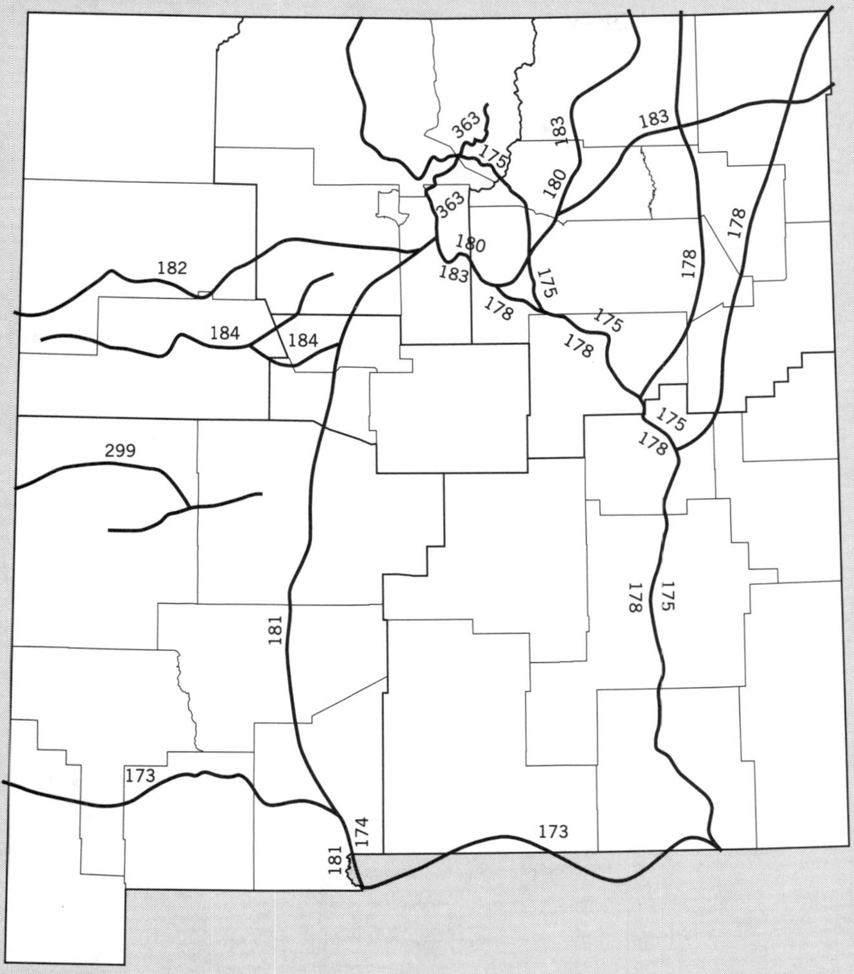
363
175
183
180
183
363
180
183
178
178
182
184
184
175
178
175
178
175
178
299
181
178
175
173
174
181
173

Multiple Property Listings

These listings are general categories encompassing several properties that are listed on the State Register individually.

#656 Socorro Multiple Resource District
#657 Anasazi Sites within the Chacoan Interaction Sphere
#720 La Luz Townsite
#896 Historic Resources of Watrous
#1176 Anton Chico Land Grant
#1284 Historic Resources of the Downtown Neighborhoods Area of Albuquerque
#1521 Resources of the Upland Valleys of Mora County
#1534 Domestic Architecture in Socorro, New Mexico 1870-1912
#1547 Rayado Ranch of Colfax County
#1550 Pueblo IV Sites of the Chupadera Arroyo
#1564 Historic and Architectural Resources of Route 66 through New Mexico MPS
#1582 Historic Resources of the Santa Fe Trail, 1821-1880
#1597 Mining Sites in the Nogal Mining District of the Lincoln National Forest
#1600 Architectural and Historic Resources of Hillsboro, New Mexico
#1615 Religious Properties of New Mexico
#1617 Architectural and Historic Resources of the New Deal in New Mexico
#1649 Historic Resources of Roswell, New Mexico
#1661 Historic Highway Bridges of New Mexico
#1687 Auto-oriented Commercial Development in Albuquerque 1916-1956
#1698 Historic Resources of Magdalena
#1699 Historic Resources of Albuquerque's North Valley
#1700 Large Pueblo Sites Near Jemez Springs, New Mexico
#1701 Red River Multiple Resource Area
#1702 Artificial Stone Houses of Artesia
#1703 Late Prehistoric Cultural Developments along the Rio Chama and Tributaries
#1704 Historic U.S. Post Offices in New Mexico, 1900-1941
#1705 Historic Resources of La Tierra Amarilla
#1706 Prehistoric and Historic Agricultural Sites in the Lower Rio Bonito Valley
#1707 New Mexico Campus Buildings Built 1906-1937
#1708 National Forest Fire Lookouts in the Southwestern Region
#1710 Corona Phase Sites in the Jicarilla Mountains
#1711 Prehistoric Adaptations along the Rio Grande Drainage, Sierra County, New Mexico
#1712 Homesteads on the Lincoln National Forest, New Mexico
#1714 Historic Resources of the Mimbres Valley
#1715 Historic Resources of Las Vegas, New Mexico
#1716 Historic Resources of Aztec
#1718 Navajo/Refugee Pueblo Thematic Group

#1719 Animas Phase Sites in Hidalgo County
#1720 Rio Medio Archaeological Thematic Group
#1721 Anasazi Communities of the Cibolan Culture Area, West Central New Mexico
#1722 County Courthouses of New Mexico
#1723 Prehistoric Communities of the La Plata Valley
#1724 Historic Resources of Downtown Gallup
#1725 Chaco Mesa Pueblo III
#1727 Gallina Cultural Developments in North-Central New Mexico
#1728 Jemez Culture Developments in North Central New Mexico
#1729 Lincoln Phase Sites in the Sierra Blanca Region
#1730 Railroad Logging Sites of the Sacramento Mountains
#1731 Ring Midden Sites of the Guadalupe Mountains, New Mexico (AD 700-1900)
#1737 Public Works of the CCC in the Lincoln National Forest
#1751 Archaic Sites of the Northwest Jemez Mountains
#1755 Rockshelter Sites of the Western Escarpment of the Sacramento Mountain
#1758 Cultural Developments on the Pajarito Plateau
#1766 Railroad Logging Era Resources of the Canon de San Diego Land Grant in North Central New Mexico
#1772 Historic Resources of Downtown Deming

PHOTO CREDITS

Cover:

TOP LEFT: Carlsbad Caverns National Park Historic District. *Photo by Marci L. Riskin*

MIDDLE LEFT: Aztec Ruins National Monument. *Photo by Betsy Swanson*

BOTTOM LEFT: San Jose de Gracia Church and Collections. *Photo by Marci L. Riskin*

TOP RIGHT: Wagon Mound. *Photo by Richard Federici*

BOTTOM RIGHT: Santa Rita Copper Mines Historic Site. *HPD File Photo*

Contents:
Photo by Betsy Swanson

Foreword:
HPD File Photo

Page 13:
Photo by John Conran

Northwest

p. 20 Richard Federici
p. 21 Betsy Swanson
p. 22 HPD File Photo
p. 26 Larry L. Baker
p. 27 HPD File Photo
p. 29 HPD File Photo
p. 30 Betsy Swanson

North-Central

p. 36 HPD File Photo
p. 38 William Stone
p. 39 David Kammer
p. 41 Richard Federici
p. 43 Betsy Swanson
p. 44 HPD File Photo
p. 45 HPD File Photo
p. 48 l Richard Federici
p. 48 r Marci L. Riskin
p. 49 l Kristina Kershner
p. 49 r Richard Federici
p. 51 Robert Tórrez
p. 52 Betsy Swanson
p. 54 Marci L. Riskin
p. 55 Bill Pickens
p. 56 l HPD File Photo
p. 56 r Marci L. Riskin
p. 58 HPD File Photo
p. 59 Alan Stoker
p. 60 Marci L. Riskin
p. 61 Marci L. Riskin
p. 63 Marci L. Riskin
p. 64 National Park Service, Fred Mang, Jr.
p. 65 HPD File Photo
p. 66 Marci L. Riskin
p. 67 Marci L. Riskin
p. 68 Richard Federici

Northeast

p. 70 Karl Kernberger
p. 72 l Karl Kernberger
p. 72 r Gregory M. Franzwa
p. 73 Kristina Kershner
p. 75 HPD File Photo
p. 77 Richard Federici
p. 79 HPD File Photo
p. 82 HPD File Photo
p. 84 National Park Service, Fred Mang, Jr.
p. 85 HPD File Photo
p. 86 HPD File Photo
p. 88 David Kammer
p. 89 Marci L. Riskin
p. 90 Richard Federici
p. 91 Charlie Steen

Central

p. 92 John Conran
p. 93 James D. Hinde
p. 97 HPD File Photo
p. 99 Richard Federici
p. 100 HPD File Photo
p. 102 Marci L. Riskin
p. 104 Marci L. Riskin
p. 107 HPD File Photo
p. 108 David Kammer

Southwest

p. 111 HPD File Photo
p. 112 White Sands Missile Range
p. 113 Richard Federici
p. 114 HPD File Photo
p. 116 Barbara Zook
p. 117 HPD File Photo
p. 118 HPD File Photo
p. 119 HPD File Photo
p. 120 l Betsy Swanson
p. 120 r Marci L. Riskin
p. 122 Betsy Swanson
p. 123 Richard Federici
p. 124 Karl Kernberger
p. 125 HPD File Photo
p. 126 HPD File Photo
p. 128 HPD File Photo
p. 129 Marci L. Riskin
p. 130 Marci L. Riskin
p. 131 Marci L. Riskin
p. 133 Marci L. Riskin
p. 136 Marci L. Riskin

Southeast

p. 138 Lincoln National Forest
p. 140 t HPD File Photo
p. 140 b Marci L. Riskin
p. 141 Betsy Swanson
p. 142 HPD File Photo
p. 143 Betsy Swanson
p. 144 Marci L. Riskin
p. 145 HPD File Photo
p. 146 Marci L. Riskin
p. 147 Wendell Bell
p. 148 HPD File Photo
p. 149 Marci L. Riskin
p. 150 Marci L. Riskin
p. 151 Betsy Swanson
p. 152 Betsy Swanson
p. 153 Karl Kernberger

INDEX OF HIGHLIGHTED PROPERTIES